*f*P

Tattoos on the Heart

The Power of Boundless Compassion

Gregory Boyle

Free Press

New York   London   Toronto   Sydney

Free Press

A Division of Simon & Schuster, Inc.

1230 Avenue of the Americas

New York, NY 10020

First Free Press hardcover edition March 2010

FREE PRESS and colophon are trademarks of Simon & Schuster, Inc.

For information about special discounts for bulk purchases, please contact Simon & Schuster Special Sales at 1-866-506-1949 or business@simonandschuster.com.

The Simon & Schuster Speakers Bureau can bring authors to your live event. For more information or to book an event contact the Simon & Schuster Speakers Bureau at 1-866-248-3049 or visit our website at www.simonspeakers.com.

Manufactured in the United States of America

1   3   5   7   9   10   8   6   4   2

Library of Congress Cataloging-in-Publication Data

Boyle, Greg.

Tattoos on the heart : the power of boundless compassion / Gregory Boyle.

p. cm.

1. Christian life—Anecdotes.   2. Church work.

3. Boyle, Greg.   I. Title.

BV4517.B665 2010

277.94'94083—dc22   2009032970

ISBN 978-1-4391-5302-4

ISBN 978-1-4391-7177-6 (ebook)

Chapter Nine, "Kinship," appeared in slightly different form in *The Homeboy Review,* April 2009.

The author is donating 100 percent of his net proceeds from the book to Homeboy Industries. Homeboy Industries assists at-risk and formerly gang-involved youth to become positive and contributing members of society through job placement, training, and education.

To the Homies and the Homegirls

Contents

"This day . . . with me . . . paradise."

—Luke 23:43

Preface

I suppose I've tried to write this book for more than a decade. People encouraged me all the time, but I never felt I had the discipline (or blocks of time) to do it. I have all these stories and parables locked away in the "Public Storage" of my brain, and I have long wanted to find a permanent home for them. The usual "containers" for these stories are my homilies at Mass in the twenty-five detention centers where I celebrate the Eucharist (juvenile halls, probation camps, and Youth Authority facilities). I illustrate the gospel with three stories and usually tell another one just before communion. After Mass once, at one of these probation camps, a homie grabbed both my hands and looked me in the eye. "This is my last Mass at camp. I go home on Monday. I'm gonna miss your stories. You tell good stories. And I hope . . . I never have to hear your stories again."

Along with my ministry in jails, I give nearly two hundred talks a year to social workers, law enforcement, university students, parish groups, and educators. The stories get trotted out there too. They are the bricks around which I hope, in this book, to slather some thematic mortar that can hold them together. With any luck, they will lift us up so we can see beyond the confines of the things that limit our view. After recently bumping heads with cancer, I started to feel that death might actually *not* make an exception in my case. So sensing that none of us will get out of this alive, I asked for and was graciously given a four-month sabbatical by my provincial superior, John McGarry, S.J., and sent to Italy. This will explain the *ragu de agnello* stains on some of the pages that follow.

There are several things this book knows it doesn't want to be. It's not a memoir of my past twenty plus years working with gang members. There is no narrative chronology that I'll follow, though I will give a brief aerial view of Dolores Mission and the birth and beginnings of Homeboy Industries. The subsequent stories will need that kind of contextualizing "at the gate" (as the homies say), if they are to make sense. I would refer the reader to an excellent account of those early days at Dolores Mission in Celeste Fremon's *G-Dog and the Homeboys*. Her keen portrayal of the young men and women who struggled with this gang phenomenon in the early '90s in that community has now become an even more powerful, longitudinal study in the sociology of gangs, with her two recent updates of the material. (Young gang members write me from all over the country, after having read Celeste's book, and have been deeply moved by it. Most say it's the only book they have, thus far, ever read.)

My book will not be a "How to deal with gangs" book. It will not lay out a comprehensive plan for a city to prevent and intervene·in their burgeoning gang situation.

Clearly, the themes that bind the stories together are things that matter to me. As a Jesuit for thirty-seven years and a priest for twenty-five years, it would not be possible for me to present these stories apart from God, Jesus, compassion, kinship, redemption, mercy, and our common call to delight in one another. If there is a fundamental challenge within these stories, it is simply to change our lurking suspicion that some lives matter less than other lives. William Blake wrote, "We are put on earth for a little space that we might learn to bear the beams of love." Turns out this is what we all have in common, gang member and nongang member alike: we're just trying to learn how to bear the beams of love.

A note on how I've chosen to proceed. In virtually every instance, I have changed the names of the young men and women whose stories fill these pages, with the exception of anecdotes in which the name is the subject of the story. I have also foregone mentioning any specific gang by its name. Too much heartache, pain, and death have been visited upon our communities to elevate these groupings to any possible fame these pages could bring them. Everything in this book happened, as best as I can recall. I apologize, *antemano*, if I have left out some detail, person, or subtle contour that those familiar with these stories would have included.

I was born and raised in the "gang capital of the world," Los Angeles, California, just west of the area where I have spent nearly a quarter of a century in ministry. I had two wonderful parents, five sisters and two brothers, lived comfortably, went to Catholic private schools, and always had jobs once I was of an age to work. Disneyland was not the "Happiest Place on Earth"; my home on Norton Avenue was. As a teenager, though, I would not have known a gang member if one came up and, as they say, "hit me upside the head." I would not have been able to find a gang if you'd sent me on a scavenger hunt to locate one. It is safe to declare that as a teenager growing up in LA, it would have been impossible for me to join a gang. That is a fact. That fact, however, does not make me morally superior to the young men and women you will meet in this book. Quite the opposite. I have come to see with greater clarity that the day simply won't come when I am more noble, have more courage, or am closer to God than the folks whose lives fill these pages.

In Africa they say "a person becomes a person through other people." There can be no doubt that the homies have returned me to myself. I've learned, with their patient guidance, to worship Christ as He lives in them. It's easy to echo Gerard Manley Hopkins here, "For I greet him the days I meet him, and bless when I understand."

Once, after dealing with a particularly exasperating homie named Sharkey, I switch my strategy and decide to catch him in the act of doing the right thing. I can see I have been too harsh and exacting with him, and he is, after all, trying the best he can. I tell him how heroic he is and how the courage he now exhibits in transforming his life far surpasses the hollow "bravery" of his barrio past. I tell him that he is a giant among men. I mean it. Sharkey seems to be thrown off balance by all this and silently stares at me. Then he says, "Damn, G . . . I'm gonna tattoo that on my heart."

In finding a home for these stories in this modest effort, I hope, likewise, to tattoo those mentioned here on our collective heart. Though this book does not concern itself with solving the gang problem, it does aspire to broaden the parameters of our kinship. It hopes not only to put a human face on the gang member, but to recognize our own wounds in the broken lives and daunting struggles of the men and women in these parables.

Our common human hospitality longs to find room for those

who are left out. It's just who we are if allowed to foster something different, something more greatly resembling what God had in mind. Perhaps, together, we can teach each other how to bear the beams of love, persons becoming persons, right before our eyes. Returned to ourselves.

Tattoos on the Heart

Introduction

Dolores Mission and Homeboy Industries

I spent the summers of 1984 and 1985 as an associate pastor at Dolores Mission Church, the poorest parish in the Los Angeles archdiocese. In 1986 I became pastor of the church. Originally, I was scheduled to go to Santa Clara University to run their student service program, but Bolivia changed all that. I can't explain how the poor in Bolivia evangelized me during that year of 1984–85, but they turned me inside out, and from that moment forward I only wanted to walk with them. This was a wholly selfish decision on my part. I knew that the poor had some privileged delivery system for giving me access to the gospel. Naturally, I wanted to be around this. When I raised this desire to work with the poor with my provincial superior, I was sent to Dolores Mission, instead of Santa Clara, as the youngest pastor in the history of the diocese. The church had been in Boyle Heights for some forty years, nestled in the middle of two large public-housing projects, Pico Gardens and Aliso Village. Together, they comprised the largest grouping of public housing west of the Mississippi. When I arrived, we had eight active gangs, seven Latino and one African American. (The projects were 25 percent African American back in 1986 and are now 99.9 percent Latino.) At the time, the Pico-Aliso area was known to have the highest concentration of gang activity in the entire city. If Los Angeles was the gang capital of the world, our little postage-stamp-size area on the map was the gang capital of LA. I buried my first young person killed because of gang violence in 1988, and as of this writing, I have been called upon for this sad task an additional 167 times.

The first kid I buried was an eighteen-year-old identical twin. Even the family had a hard time distinguishing these two brothers from each other. At the funeral, Vicente peered into the casket of his brother, Danny. They were both wearing identical clothes. It was as if someone had slapped a mirror down and Vicente was staring at his own reflection. Because this was my first funeral of this kind, the snapshot of a young man peering at his own mirror image has stayed with me all these years, as a metaphor for gang violence in all its self-destruction.

At the time, there were so many gang-involved middle school kids who had been given "the boot" from their schools that their constant presence in the projects during school hours brought violence and major drug-dealing. So the first thing we did as a parish community, to respond to this gang reality, was to open our alternative school, Dolores Mission Alternative (DMA), in 1988. The school drew different gangs and their members to the third floor of Dolores Mission's elementary school in what used to be the convent. Fights were daily occurrences and keeping staff was a challenge. We had a principal last two days and several teachers who hung in there for just one.

With the school came a new parish attitude. Suddenly, the welcome mat was tentatively placed out front. A new sense of "church" had emerged, open and inclusive, replacing the hermetically sealed model that had kept the "good folks" in and the "bad folks" out. The Christian Base Communities (*Comunidades Eclesiales de Base*—CEBs) were sectors of people in the parish, mainly women, who reflected on the gospel as it impacted their real lives. Their reflection compelled them to extend themselves to the gangs in their area of the projects. They would have *carne asadas* and other gatherings to communicate clearly that the gang members were not our enemies. One CEB even had a Thanksgiving dinner for homies who had no place to go. They wanted to signal to the gang members, "You are our sons/daughters—whether we brought you into this world or not."

I can remember standing outside police tape on an early Sunday morning, just around the block from the church. The body of a gang member was lying on the ground, partially covered with a sheet. His head and upper torso were draped with the sheet, revealing only his oversize, cut-off Dickies shorts, white tube socks pulled up to the knee, and a pair of blue Nike Cortez—all standard-issue gang wear at the time. He wasn't from the projects, and who knows why he wandered into this foreign turf. Pam McDuffy, an activist mother in the community, sidled up to me and put her arm around my waist. She was crying. "I don't know who that kid is, but he was some mother's son."

Soon gang members began to "kick it" at the church. The garage became a quasi-weight room, and the bell tower always had some ten gang members or so huddled there, smoking cigarettes and passing the time. I figured if they're at the church, they're not wreaking havoc in the community. This didn't thrill all parishioners, and the grumbling reached a pitch that forced me to call a parish meeting. The parish hall was packed; this would be either a vote of confidence in my leadership or an opportunity for the parishioners to tell me, "Here's your hat, what's your hurry."

I didn't speak. But the "E. F. Huttons" of the community (when they spoke, people tended to listen), Teresa Navarro and Paula Hernandez, needed only to stand and invoke Jesus.

"We help gang members at this parish because it is what Jesus would do."

People applauded and the parish never looked back.

Soon the women organized major marches, or *caminatas*, moving through the projects, often in the heat of tension and in the wake of ceaseless shooting. The *Comité Pro Paz* (Committee for Peace), as the women called themselves, would move to hotspots, and their gentle praying and singing presence would calm the gang members ready for battle.

It was one such march that gave birth to Homeboy Industries in 1988. Armed with fliers reading Jobs for a Future, hundreds of women walked to the factories surrounding the housing projects and, with this show of force, handed a flier to the foreman of each factory. It had become clear that what gang members most requested were jobs. Having a *jale* (a job) was all they ever talked about. We waited for the factories to call with employment offers, but this never happened. Still, an organization was born: Jobs for a Future—which initially sought gainful employment for the gang members from Pico-Aliso.

This parish-led program soon launched projects that hired huge swaths of gang members: the building of a child-care center, neighborhood clean-up crews, and graffiti removal, landscaping, and maintenance crews. Gang members were placed in a variety of businesses and nonprofits, and Jobs for a Future paid their salaries. I wrote more rubber checks than a U.S. congressperson. We constantly lived in the paradox of precariousness. The money was never there when you needed it, and it was always on time.

It was during this period that I promoted any number of truces, cease-fires, and peace treaties. I spent a great deal of time in a kind of shuttle diplomacy, riding my bike between neighborhoods (as gang members do, I use interchangeably the words "gang," "barrio," and "neighborhood"; they all refer to "gang"), securing signed agreements from the warring factions. Some were Pyrrhic victories such as an agreement not to shoot into houses.

I learned early on that all sides would speak so positively about the peace process when first approached.

"Yeah, G [what most homies call me; short for Greg], let's get a peace treaty going."

But once you brought them together, they couldn't resist posturing in high gear in front of one another. I eventually ceased having these meetings, and like the Soviet Union and the USA, I worked out all the details of peace beforehand and just had the principals sign the agreements.

That was then; this is now. Though I don't regret having orchestrated these truces and treaties, I'd never do it again. The unintended consequence of it all was that it legitimized the gangs and fed them oxygen. I eventually came to see that this kind of work keeps gangs alive.

The unrest of 1992 was unlike anything I had ever seen in Los Angeles. Working my paper corner as a sixth grader during the

Watts riots in 1965, I had a sense then of containment—that this was unrest happening "over there."

Not so in 1992. The sky, blackened with smoke, reached every corner of the city. I sat on the stoop of an apartment in Pico Gardens with a huge gang member, a shot-caller. When all the other homies were out of earshot, he turned to me and said, "This is the end of the world, isn't it, G?" his voice trembling and uncertain.

I reassured him, "No, 'course it isn't."

But I wasn't at all sure that he was wrong. The National Guard arrived in our projects several days after the initial explosion of things, but we didn't need them there. Things didn't explode in this, the poorest of communities in Los Angeles, where everyone fully expected mayhem. I suspect the reason they didn't was that we had so many strategically employed gang members who finally had a stake in keeping the projects from igniting that the peace was kept.

Because I said as much in a *Los Angeles Times* interview about the riot, Ray Stark summoned me. Ray was a hugely successful Hollywood agent (Humphrey Bogart, Kirk Douglas) and a megahit movie producer (*Funny Girl*). His beloved wife, Fran, had died shortly before our visit, and Ray wanted to make an impact on this burgeoning and daunting gang issue. At our meeting Ray suggested some ideas that I had to respectfully dismiss. Finally, after I swatted down a number of these suggestions (e.g., arm gang members with their own video cameras so we could make a documentary), Ray was exasperated.

"I give up, what do you think I should do with my money?"

I told him that an old bakery was for sale across the street from the church. He could buy it, and we could bring rival gang members together. We could call it The Homeboy Bakery.

Ray was electrified, and so we began the economic-development branch of Jobs for a Future. Some months later, we commandeered a tortilla machine in the Grand Central Market, and now, with multiple businesses, we became Homeboy Industries (no longer Jobs for a Future) in the summer of 1992.

Our first office was on the church property, but our second was a storefront at 1848 East First Street, from 1994 to 2000. White Memorial Hospital, long supporters of my work with gang members, paid my rent. It was here that gang members from all the forty-plus gangs in the Hollenbeck Police Division (some ten thousand members) began to arrive, looking for a way out of the gang life. Perhaps gang members had always longed for this, but for the absence of a place to go, the desire had festered. Soon we added staff and job developers to locate employment in the private sector. We began tattoo removal because of a guy named Ramiro. A gang member, fresh out of prison, with a long record, had FUCK THE WORLD tattooed on his forehead, completely filling the space there. He told me his job search was not going so great. I'm only imagining him at McDonald's: "Do you want fries with that?" and seeing mothers grab their kids, fleeing the store.

So I hired him at the bakery, and little by little we erased his forehead. We have since added many laser machines and doctors who perform more than four thousand treatments a year.

We owe it all to Ramiro (who moved on to a job as a security guard at a movie studio—no trace left of the angriest moment in his life).

Businesses have come and gone at Homeboy Industries. We

have had starts and stops, but anything worth doing is worth failing at. We started Homeboy Plumbing. That didn't go so well. Who knew? People didn't want gang members in their homes. I just didn't see that coming.

At the turn of the century, we needed more space, so we moved to our third headquarters up the block at 1916 East First Street, into a rehabbed printing factory. After a while, we started serving gang members outside Boyle Heights as well, and we now had a thousand folks a month, from forty-five different zip codes. Members from more than eight hundred gangs from all over the county now came seeking employment, tattoo removal, mental health counseling, case management, and legal services.

By 2007 we had so burst our seams that we built our current headquarters, Homeboy Bakery, and Homegirl Café near Chinatown in downtown Los Angeles. Our most successful business is Homeboy Silkscreen, ably run all these years by Ruben and Cristina Rodriguez, and we operate four others: Homeboy Bakery, Homeboy/Homegirl Merchandising, Homeboy Maintenance, and Homegirl Café, where women with records, young ladies from rival gangs, waitresses with attitude, will gladly take your order.

Los Angeles County claims 1,100 gangs with nearly 86,000 members. A great number of these youth know to come to Homeboy when they are ready to "hang up their gloves."

Homeboy Industries is not for those who need help, only for those who want it. In this sense, we are a gang-rehabilitation center. Often the homies who come to us are not-ready-for-prime-time players. Just released from prison, they are offered what is often their first jobs, where they glean soft skills at Homeboy

Industries like learning to show up on time, every day, and taking orders from disagreeable supervisors.

We provide all of this, free of charge. We are a worksite and therapeutic community. We are a training program and business. We are all of the above all at the same time. Once the homies come to feel some confidence in the workplace, they can move on to higher-paying opportunities elsewhere. Also, we give homies a chance to work with their enemies. The place has become the "United Nations" of gangs. When enemies work with one another, a valuable "disconnect" is created on the streets. It forces a fellow active gang member to ask the employed homie, "How can you work with that guy?" Answering that question will be awkward, clumsy, and always require courage, but the question itself jostles the status quo.

Finally, Homeboy Industries can only hire and help a finite number of gang members. Though thousands have found assistance, it remains a tiny drop in a pretty deep bucket. In the city of Los Angeles, Homeboy Industries has operated as a symbol as much as a place of concrete help. For more than twenty years, it has asked this city, "What if we were to invest in gang members, rather than just seek to incarcerate our way out of this problem?"

After two decades, the city of Los Angeles has embraced Homeboy Industries as its own and has allowed it to shape how we see this "condition" and how we can, in part, respond to it.

A homie named David who had sunk to homelessness and heroin addiction was beating himself up one day.

"Look, David," I tell him, wanting to cut his meat up for him, "You have to crawl before you can walk, and then walk before you can run."

David's eyes soften with tears. "Yeah, but I know I can fly. I just need to catch a gust o' wind."

Homeboy Industries wants to be that gust.

It's when we face for a moment the worst our kind can do, and shudder to know the taint in our own selves, that awe cracks the mind's shell and enters the heart.
—Denise Levertov

* * *

In 1992 Homeboy Bakery is launched, but seven years later, in October of 1999, it burns to the ground. I get the panicky call at three in the morning with the news. I arrive to find the bakery surrounded by fire trucks, hoses shooting water everywhere, flames stretching high. Women from the projects across the street greet me and wrap me in their arms. Tearfully, they promise that when the sun comes up, they will have a *venta de comida* and begin the fundraising.

A young girl hugs me, crying, "Don't worry, G, we'll have a car wash."

I must admit, initially, I thought it was arson. When I say this, people often presume I mean that gang members did it. I never thought that. Homeboy Bakery stood as a symbol of hope to every gang member in the county. That they would destroy this place of second chances didn't make sense.

But we had lots of enemies in those early days, folks who felt that assisting gang members somehow cosigned on their bad behavior. Hate mail, death threats, and bomb threats were

10

common, especially after I wrote Op-Ed pieces in the *Los Angeles Times* (which I had done just prior to the fire).

We used to joke during this period of hostility that emanated from those who opposed the very idea of Homeboy that with so much vitriol leveled at us, we ought to change our voice mail message after hours: "Thank you for calling Homeboy Industries. Your bomb threat is important to us."

From my office once, I heard a homegirl answer the phone, and she says to the caller, "Go ahead and bring that bomb, mutha fucka. We're ready for your ass."

I ask her who's on the phone.

She covers the receiver, nonplussed, "Oh, just some fool who wants to blow the place up."

"Uh, kiddo, um," I tell her, "Maybe we should just say, 'Have a nice day and God bless you.'"

The day of the bakery fire, within an hour of my arrival, the fire inspectors are able with certainty to deem the cause of the fire to be "natural." The place was eighty years old, after all, with wiring from *aquel tiempo*. An electrical short traveled through the walls, took a breather in the bakery's office long enough to percolate, and soon the whole place imploded.

But, of course, we don't know all this in the first half hour, and during this time of not knowing, a wizened, Irish-looking fire inspector comes over to me.

"You the owner?" he asks, flames shooting through the roof of the bakery behind him.

"Yeah."

"Um," he says, "You got any reason to believe why someone might have started this fire?"

"No."

"Uh, you didn't have any . . . uh . . . disgruntled, ex-employees, did ya?"

"No," I tell him, "All the disgruntled ones still work for me."

I needed to break the tension even if he didn't need to. He does not smile.

"You know this area, where the bakery's located?" he surveys it with a whisper, turning his head from side to side. "Well . . . it's known for hoodlums."

Like this might come as a surprise to me.

"Well," I tell him, "I think we're okay here cuz at Homeboy Industries," now I'm the one whispering, "we only hire hoodlums."

Again, no smiling.

The next day we were able to inform all the bakers what happened, but we couldn't locate one of them, a kid named Lencho. So when the time came for his shift to begin, Lencho steps off the bus, wearing his perfectly *planchado* white uniform, with the words HOMEBOY BAKERY embroidered on one side and his name, LENCHO, emblazoned on the other. His step is light as he walks to the parking lot.

But once he enters, he sees the soggy mess extracted by the firefighters. He sees smoke still wafting through the sizable hole in the roof. He sees his coworkers, all rivals from enemy gangs, picking through the rubble. No one needs to explain. He stands there frozen, puts his head in his hands, and begins to sob.

This was his reason to get up in the morning. Just as important, it was his reason not to gangbang the night before. The union he shared with his coworkers, former enemies, was deeper than anything he had ever known in his family and certainly stronger than the bond he knew in his gang. All we could do was surround him with love and the promise of rebuilding.

Ten years later, he is back, working in the brand-new bakery.

* * *

The original bakery was hugely famous from its first week. News crews would visit almost daily. Articles were written with photos of enemies working alongside one another. Tour groups came from all over the world. Busloads of Japanese tourists dropped by. Even Prince Charles's business advisors swooped down on us.

"Pip Pip Cheerio" meets the Homies.

Our foreman at the time was a man named Luis, in his mid-twenties, who arguably had been among the biggest, savviest drug dealers our community had ever known. We knew each other for more than a decade, and any offer of a job was always, graciously, but surely, declined. Luis was as smart as they come and quick-witted.

He used to say, "When we were kids, we would play Kick the Can but so did the cops. You know, they'd play Kick the Mexi-Can or Kick the PuertoRi-Can."

He never got caught. Too smart. If the cops rolled by and he was standing with me, he'd mumble, "Beam me up, Scottie." But when his daughter, Tiffany, was born, things changed. He wanted to work at the bakery, and his natural leadership abilities soon moved him up to foreman. Not only did he work with former rivals, he also supervised them, which is a great deal more difficult.

One day we received an odd request for a tour from farmers from the central valley of California. They want to see the bakery. It's part of Luis's job description to greet the busloads and the film crews. He hates this part of his job, and his whining could make your teeth ache.

"Do I gotta?"

The day the farmers arrive, he and I are waiting for the bus to pull up, and I'm swinging at his whiny complaints like a bunch of pesky gnats.

Finally, the bus drives into the awkward bakery parking lot, and I wave and direct it to its reserved spot. It's one of those ultramodern buses, sleek and slick, equipped with a microphone at the front of the bus for the tour guide.

Luis pretends he's the tour guide. "Welcome to Homeboy Bakery," his voice nasally drones with tour-guide disinterest. "Observe gang members in their natural habitat."

He is holding his fist up to his mouth, for greater amplification. "Please keep your hands in the bus at all times. Do not attempt to feed the homies. They are not yet tame."

"*Cállate, cabrón*," I say through the part of my mouth not smiling, welcoming our visitors from the farmland as they get off the bus.

Later in the day, I visit the bakery several blocks from my office. Seeing Luis triggers the memory of his earlier tour.

"*Oye,*" I ask him, "How'd the tour go?"

"Damn, G," he shakes his head, "What's up with white people anyway?"

I was actually curious as to what *was* up with us.

"I don't know, what *is* up with us?"

"I mean, damn," he says, "They always be using the word 'GREAT.'"

"We do?"

"Oh, hell yeah. Watcha. This buncha *gabachos* stroll in here and see the place, and it's all *firme* and clean and machines workin' proper, and they say, 'This place is GREAT.' And then they see the homies, *tú sabes*, enemies working together all *firme*, and they say, 'You fellas are GREAT.' Then they taste our bread and they go, 'This bread . . . it's GREAT.' I mean, damn, G, why white people always be usin' the word 'GREAT'?"

I tell him I don't know. But, trust me, every opportunity I could find after that, I tell him how 'GREAT' he is, just to mess with him a little.

Some four months later, it is nearly closing time, and I arrive at the bakery in the evening. Luis sees me in the parking lot from inside the building and rushes outside. He's excited, and yet "enthusiasm" is not ever the card with which Luis leads. He's too cool for that. He barely lets me get out of my car.

"Hey, G," he says, thrilled to see me, "You not gonna BELIEVE what happened to me yesterday after my shift."

He proceeds to tell me that, after work, he goes to pick up his four-year-old daughter, Tiffany, at the babysitter's. He puts her in the car, and they drive to their tiny apartment, where, for the first time, Luis is paying rent with honestly earned, clean money. He unlocks the front door, and Tiffany scurries in, down the hallway, and lands in their modest *sala*. She plants her feet in the living room and extends her arms and takes in the whole room with her eyes. She then declares, with an untethered smile, "This . . . is GREAT."

He turns and says to me, "I thought she was turning white on me."

He tells me that he lowers himself to her eye level, placing his hands on his knees for support.

"What's great, *mija*?"

Tiffany clutches her heart and gushes, "MY HOOOME!"

Luis seems to be unable to speak at exactly this moment. Our eyes find each other, and our souls well up, along with our eyes. We can't stop staring at each other, and tears make their way south on our faces. After what seems like longer than I'm sure it was, I break the silence.

I point at him. "You . . . did . . . this. You've never had a home in your life—now you have one. You did this. You were the biggest drug dealer in town, and you stopped and baked bread instead. You did this. You've never had a father in your life—and now you are one . . . and I hate to have to tell you . . . but . . . you're great."

And I hate to have to tell *you* this, but the first time I retrieved this story from my memory bank was to tell it at Luis's funeral. He wasn't doing anything wrong on the Wednesday afternoon he was killed. He was loading the trunk of his car, in the projects, readying himself for a camping trip with friends. Two gang members, with their faces covered, entered their "enemy's" territory, looking "for fools slippin'." They saw Luis and must have thought to themselves, *He'll do.* They walked up to him and executed him.

I told the "Great" story at Luis's funeral largely because of the questions I had been repeatedly asked by his friends and homies during the week that spanned his death and his burial.

"What's the point," they'd ask, "of doing good . . . If this can happen to ya?"

It was a good question, worthy of a response. I told that packed church that Luis was a human being who came to know the truth about himself and liked what he found there.

Julian of Norwich, a fourteenth-century female English

mystic, saw the life struggle as coming to discover that we are "clothed in God's goodness."

This became Luis's life's work. He embraced this goodness—his greatness—and nothing was the same again. And, really, what is death compared to knowing that? No bullet can pierce it.

With That Moon Language

Admit something:
Everyone you see, you say to them,
    "Love me."
Of course you do not do this out loud;
    Otherwise,
Someone would call the cops.
Still though, think about this,
This great pull in us to connect.
Why not become the one
Who lives with a full moon in each eye
That is always saying
With that sweet moon
    Language
What every other eye in this world
    Is dying to
    Hear.

—Hafez

1

God, I Guess

God can get tiny, if we're not careful. I'm certain we all have an image of God that becomes the touchstone, the controlling principle, to which we return when we stray.

My touchstone image of God comes by way of my friend and spiritual director, Bill Cain, S.J. Years ago he took a break from his own ministry to care for his father as he died of cancer. His father had become a frail man, dependent on Bill to do everything for him. Though he was physically not what he had been, and the disease was wasting him away, his mind remained alert and lively. In the role reversal common to adult children who care for their dying parents, Bill would put his father to bed and then read him to sleep, exactly as his father had done for him in childhood. Bill would read from some novel, and his father would lie there, staring at his son, smiling. Bill was exhausted from the day's care and work and would plead with his dad, "Look, here's the idea. I read to you, you fall asleep." Bill's father would impishly apologize and dutifully close his eyes. But this wouldn't last long.

19

Soon enough, Bill's father would pop one eye open and smile at his son. Bill would catch him and whine, "Now, come on." The father would, again, oblige, until he couldn't anymore, and the other eye would open to catch a glimpse of his son. This went on and on, and after his father's death, Bill knew that this evening ritual was really a story of a father who just couldn't take his eyes off his kid. How much more so God? Anthony De Mello writes, "Behold the One beholding you, and smiling."

God would seem to be too occupied in being unable to take Her eyes off of us to spend any time raising an eyebrow in disapproval. What's true of Jesus is true for us, and so this voice breaks through the clouds and comes straight at us. "You are my Beloved, in whom I am wonderfully pleased." There is not much "tiny" in that.

* * *

In 1990 the television news program *60 Minutes* came to Dolores Mission Church. One of its producers had read a Sunday *Los Angeles Times Magazine* article about my work with gang members in the housing projects. Mike Wallace, also seeing the piece, wanted to do a report. I was assured that I'd be getting "Good Mike." These were the days when the running joke was "you know you're going to have a bad day when Mike Wallace and a *60 Minutes* film crew show up at your office."

Wallace arrived at the poorest parish in Los Angeles in the stretchest of white limousines, stepped out of the car, wearing a flak jacket, covered with pockets, prepared, I suppose, for a journey into the jungle.

For all his initial insensitivity, toward the end of the visit, in a moment unrecorded, Wallace did say to me, "Can I admit something? I came here expecting monsters. But that's not what I found."

Later, in a recorded moment, we are sitting in a classroom filled with gang members, all students in our Dolores Mission Alternative School. Wallace points at me and says, "You won't turn these guys in to the police." Which seems quite silly to me at the time. I say something lame like, "I didn't take my vows to the LAPD." But then Wallace turns to a homie and grills him on this, saying over and over, "He won't turn you in, will he?" And then he asks the homie, "Why is that? Why do you think he won't turn you over to the police?" The kid just stares at Mike Wallace, shrugs, nonplussed, and says, "God . . . I guess."

This is a chapter on God, I guess. Truth be told, the whole book is. Not much in my life makes any sense outside of God. Certainly, a place like Homeboy Industries is all folly and bad business unless the core of the endeavor seeks to imitate the kind of God one ought to believe in. In the end, I am helpless to explain why anyone would accompany those on the margins were it not for some anchored belief that the Ground of all Being thought this was a good idea.

*　*　*

Rascal is not one to take advice. He can be recalcitrant, defensive, and primed for the fight. Well into his thirties, he's a survivor. His truck gets filled with scrap metal and with this, somehow, he feeds his kids and manages to stay on this side of eviction. To his credit, he bid prison time and gang-banging good-bye a long time ago. Rascal sometimes hits me up for funds, and I oblige if I have it *and* if his attitude doesn't foul my mood too much. But you can't tell him anything—except this one day, he actually listens. I am going on about something—can't remember what but I can see he's listening. When I'm done, he says simply, "You know, I'm gonna take that advice, and I'm gonna let it marinate," pointing at his heart, "right here."

Perhaps we should all marinate in the intimacy of God. Genesis, I suppose, got it right—"In the beginning, God." Ignatius of Loyola, the founder of the Jesuits, also spoke about the task of marinating in the "God who is always greater."

He writes, "Take care always to keep before your eyes, first, God." The secret, of course, of the ministry of Jesus, was that God was at the center of it. Jesus chose to marinate in the God who is always greater than our tiny conception, the God who "loves without measure and without regret." To anchor yourself in this, to keep always before your eyes this God is to choose to be intoxicated, marinated in the fullness of God. An Algerian Trappist, before his martyrdom, spoke to this fullness: "When you fill my heart, my eyes overflow."

* * *

Willy crept up on me from the driver's side. I had just locked the office and was ready to head home at 8:00 p.m.

"Shit, Willy," I say, "Don't be doin' that."

"'*Spensa,* G," he says, "My bad. It's just . . . well, my stomach's on *échale*. Kick me down with twenty bones, yeah?"

"Dog, my wallet's on *échale*," I tell him. A "dog" is the one upon whom you can rely—the role-dog, the person who has your back. "But get in. Let's see if I can trick any funds outta the ATM."

Willy hops on board. He is a life force of braggadocio and posturing—a thoroughly good soul—but his confidence is outsize, that of a lion wanting you to know he just swallowed a man whole. A gang member, but a peripheral one at best—he wants more to regale you with his exploits than to actually be in the midst of any. In his midtwenties, Willy is a charmer, a quintessential homie con man who's apt to coax money out of your ATM if you let him. This night, I'm tired and I want to go home.

It's easier not to resist. The Food 4 Less on Fourth and Soto has the closest ATM. I tell Willy to stay in the car, in case we run into one of Willy's rivals inside.

"Stay here, dog," I tell him, "I'll be right back."

I'm not ten feet away when I hear a muffled "Hey."

It's Willy, and he's miming, "the keys," from the passenger seat of my car. He's making over-the-top, key-in-the-ignition *señales*.

"The radio," he mouths, as he holds a hand, cupping his ear.

I wag a finger, "No, *chale*." Then it's my turn to mime. I hold both my hands together and enunciate exaggeratedly, *"Pray."*

Willy sighs and levitates his eyeballs. But he's putty. He assumes the praying hands pose and looks heavenward—*cara santucha*. I proceed on my quest to the ATM but feel the need to check in on Willy only ten yards later.

I turn and find him still in the prayer position, seeming to be only half-aware that I'm looking in on him.

I return to the car, twenty dollars in hand, and get in. Something has happened here. Willy is quiet, reflective, and there is a palpable sense of peace in the vehicle. I look at Willy and say, "You prayed, didn't you?"

He doesn't look at me. He's still and quiet. "Yeah, I did."

I start the car.

"Well, what did God say to you?" I ask him.

"Well, first He said, '*Shut up and listen.*'"

"So what d'ya do?"

"Come on, G," he says, "What am I sposed ta do? I shut up and listened."

I begin to drive him home to the barrio. I've never seen Willy like this. He's quiet and humble—no need to convince me of anything or talk me out of something else.

"So, son, tell me something," I ask. "How do you see God?"

"God?" he says, "That's my dog right there."

"And God?" I ask, "How does God see you?"

Willy doesn't answer at first. So I turn and watch as he rests his head on the recliner, staring at the ceiling of my car. A tear falls down his cheek. Heart full, eyes overflowing. "God . . . thinks . . . I'm . . . *firme.*"

To the homies, *firme* means, "could not be one bit better."

Not only does God think we're *firme*, it is God's joy to have us marinate in that.

* * *

The poet Kabir asks, "What is God?" Then he answers his own question: "God is the breath inside the breath."

Willy found his way inside the breath and it was *firme*.

I came late to this understanding in my own life—helped along by the grace-filled pedagogy of the people of Dolores

Mission. I was brought up and educated to give assent to certain propositions. God is love, for example. You concede "God loves us," and yet there is this lurking sense that perhaps you aren't fully part of the "us." The arms of God reach to embrace, and somehow you feel yourself just outside God's fingertips.

Then you have no choice but to consider that "God loves me," yet you spend much of your life unable to shake off what feels like God only embracing you begrudgingly and reluctantly. I suppose, if you insist, God has to love me too. Then who can explain this next moment, when the utter fullness of God rushes in on you—when you completely know the One in whom "you move and live and have your being," as St. Paul writes. You see, then, that it has been God's joy to love you all along. And this is completely new.

Every time one of the Jesuits at Dolores Mission would celebrate a birthday, the same ritual would repeat itself. "You know," one of the other Jesuits would say to me, for example, "Your birthday is Wednesday. The people are throwing a 'surprise party' for you on the Saturday before." The protests are as predictable as the festivities.

"Oh come on," I'd say, "Can't we pass this year?"

"Look," one of my brothers would say to me, "This party is not for you—it's for the people."

And so I am led into the parish hall for some bogus meeting, and I can hear the people "shushing" one another—*El Padre ya viene.* As I step in the door, lights go on, people shout, mariachis strike themselves up. I am called upon to muster up the same award-winning look of shock from last year. They know that you know. They don't care. They don't just love you—it's their joy to love you.

The poet Rumi writes, "Find the real world, give it endlessly away, grow rich flinging gold to all who ask. Live at the empty heart of paradox. I'll dance there with you—cheek to cheek."

Dancing *cumbias* with the women of Dolores Mission rhymes with God's own wild desire to dance with each one of us cheek to cheek.

Meister Eckhart says "God is greater than God." The hope is that our sense of God will grow as expansive as our God is. Each tiny conception gets obliterated as we discover more and more the God who is always greater.

* * *

At Camp Paige, a county detention facility near Glendora, I was getting to know fifteen-year-old Rigo, who was about to make his first communion. The Catholic volunteers had found him a white shirt and black tie. We still had some fifteen minutes before the other incarcerated youth would join us for Mass in the gym, and I'm asking Rigo the basic stuff about his family and his life. I ask about his father.

"Oh," he says, "he's a heroin addict and never really been in my life. Used to always beat my ass. Fact, he's in prison right now. Barely ever lived with us."

Then something kind of snaps in him—an image brings him to attention.

"I think I was in the fourth grade," he begins. "I came home. Sent home in the middle of the day. Got into some *pedo* at school. Can't remember what. When I got home, my *jefito* was there. He was hardly ever there. My dad says, 'Why they send you home?' And cuz my dad always beat me, I said, 'If I tell you, promise you won't hit me?' He just said, 'I'm your father. 'Course I'm not gonna hit you.' So I told him."

Rigo is caught short in the telling. He begins to cry, and in moments he's wailing and rocking back and forth. I put my arm around him. He is inconsolable. When he is able to speak and barely so, he says only, "He beat me with a pipe . . . with . . . a pipe."

When Rigo composes himself, I ask, "And your mom?" He points some distance from where we are to a tiny woman standing by the gym's entrance.

"That's her over there." He pauses for a beat, "There's no one like her." Again, some slide appears in his mind, and a thought occurs.

"I've been locked up for more than a year and a half. She comes to see me every Sunday. You know how many buses she takes every Sunday—to see my sorry ass?"

Then quite unexpectedly he sobs with the same ferocity as before. Again, it takes him some time to reclaim breath and an ability to speak. Then he does, gasping through his tears. "Seven buses. She takes . . . seven . . . buses. Imagine."

How, then, to imagine, the expansive heart of this God— greater than God—who takes seven buses, just to arrive at us. We settle sometimes for less than intimacy with God when all God longs for *is* this solidarity with us. In Spanish, when you speak of your great friend, you describe the union and kinship as being *de uña y mugre*—our friendship is like the fingernail and the dirt under it. Our image of who God is and what's on God's mind is more tiny than it is troubled. It trips more on our puny sense of God than over conflicting creedal statements or theological considerations.

The desire of God's heart is immeasurably larger than our

imaginations can conjure. This longing of God's to give us peace and assurance and a sense of well-being only awaits our willingness to cooperate with God's limitless magnanimity.

* * *

"Behold the One beholding you and smiling." It is precisely because we have such an overactive disapproval gland ourselves that we tend to create God in our own image. It is truly hard for us to see the truth that disapproval does not seem to be part of God's DNA. God is just too busy loving us to have any time left for disappointment.

* * *

One day I receive a phone call in my office around three in the afternoon. It's from a twenty-five-year-old homie named Cesar. I have known him for most of his life. I can remember first meeting him when he was a little kid in Pico Gardens during the earthquake of 1987 when the projects had become a tent city. People lived outside in *carpas* well past the time of any danger. Cesar was one of the many kids seeking reassurance from me.

"Are we gonna be okay? Is this the end of the world?"

I spent every evening of those two weeks walking the tents, and I always associate Cesar with that period.

He's calling me today because he has just finished a four-year stint in prison. Turned out, earthquakes were the least of Cesar's troubles. He had joined the local gang, since there wasn't anyone around to "chase his ass" and rein him in. At this point in his life, Cesar had been locked up more often than not. Cesar and I chitchat on the phone, dispatching the niceties in short order—"It's good to be out—I'd love to see ya"—then Cesar says, "Let me just cut to the cheese."

This was not a spin I had heard on this expression before.

"You know, I just got outta the *pinta* and don't really have a place to stay. Right now, I'm staying with a friend in his apartment—here in El Monte—away from the projects and the hood and the homies. *Y sabes qué*, I don't got no clothes. My lady she left me, and she burned all my clothes, you know, in some anger toward me, I guess."

I'm waiting for him to cut to the cheese.

"So I don't got no clothes," he says. "Can you help me?"

"Sure, son," I say, "Look, it's three now. I'll pick you up after work, at six o'clock."

I drive to the apartment at the appointed hour, and I'm surprised to see Cesar standing on the sidewalk waiting for me—I'm used to searching for homies when asked to retrieve them. I guess you might say that Cesar is a scary-looking guy. It's not just the fact that he's large and especially, fresh out of prison, newly "swole" from lifting weights. He exudes menace. So there he is, standing and waiting for me. When he sees it's me, this huge ex-con does this bouncing up and down, yippy-skippy, happy-to-see-ya, hand-clapping gleeful jig.

He flies into my car and throws his arms around me. "When I saw you right now, G, I got aaaallllll happy!"

There was some essence to him that hadn't changed from that child wanting to know that the world was safe from earthquakes.

We go to JCPenney, and I tell him he can buy two hundred dollars' worth of clothes. In no time, his arms are filled with the essentials, and we both are standing in a considerable line to pay for it all. All the other customers are staring at Cesar. Not only is he menacing, but he seems to have lost his volume knob. People can't help but turn and look, though they all take great pains to pretend they're not listening.

"Hey," he says, in what you might call a loud-ass voice, "See dat couple over there?"

I am not the only one turning and looking. The entire check-out line shifts. Cesar points to a young couple with a tiny son.

"Well, I walk up to that guy and I look at him and I say, 'Hey, don't I know you?' And his *ruca* grabs the *morrito* and holds him and shakes her head and says, 'NO, WE DON'T KNOW YOU!' all *panickeada así*. Then the *vato* looks at me like he's gonna have a damn *paro cardiaco*, and *he* shakes his head, 'NO, I DON'T KNOW YOU.' Then I look at him more closer, and I say, 'Oh, my bad, I thought you were somebody else.' And they get aaaaallllll relaxed when I say that." He takes a breath. "I mean, damn, G . . . do I look *that* scary?"

I shake my head no and say, "Yeah, pretty much, dog."

The customers can't help themselves, and we all laugh.

I drop Cesar off at his friend's apartment. He becomes quiet and vulnerable, as frightened as a child displaced by shifting ground.

"I just don't want to go back. *La neta*, I'm scared."

"Look, son," I say to him, "Who's got a better heart than you? And God is at the center of that great, big ol' heart. Hang on to that, dog—cuz you have what the world wants. So, what can go wrong?"

We say our good-byes, and as I watch him walk away alone, I find his gentleness and disarming sweet soul a kind of elixir, soothing my own doubts and calling me to fearlessness.

At three o'clock in the morning, the phone rings. It's Cesar. He says what every homie says when they call in the middle of the night, "Did I wake you?"

I always think *Why no, I was just waiting and hoping that you'd call.*

Cesar is sober, and it's urgent that he talk to me.

"I gotta ask you a question. You know how I've always seen you as my father—ever since I was a little kid? Well, I hafta ask you a question."

Now Cesar pauses, and the gravity of it all makes his voice waver and crumble, "Have I . . . been . . . your son?"

"Oh, hell, yeah," I say.

"Whew," Cesar exhales, "I thought so."

Now his voice becomes enmeshed in a cadence of gentle sobbing. "Then . . . I will be . . . your son. And you . . . will be my father. And nothing will separate us, right?"

"That's right."

In this early morning call Cesar did not discover that he has a father. He discovered that he is a son worth having. The voice broke through the clouds of his terror and the crippling mess of his own history, and he felt himself beloved. God, wonderfully pleased in him, is where God wanted Cesar to reside.

Jesus, in Matthew's gospel, says, "How narrow is the gate that leads to life." Mistakenly, I think, we've come to believe that this is about restriction. The way is narrow. But it really wants us to see that narrowness *is* the way.

St. Hedwig writes, "All is narrow for me, I feel so vast." It's about funneling ourselves into a central place. Our choice is not to focus on the narrow, but to narrow our focus. The gate that leads to life is not about restriction at all. It is about an entry

31

into the expansive. There is a vastness in knowing you're a son/daughter worth having. We see our plentitude in God's own expansive view of us, and we marinate in this.

*   *   *

In March of 2004, Scrappy walks into our office and, I'm not proud to admit it, my heart sinks. From the perch of my own glass-enclosed office, I can see Scrappy talking to Marcos, the receptionist, who is also from Scrappy's gang. He is apparently signing up to see me. I haven't seen Scrappy in ten years, since he's been incarcerated all that time, but even before that, I'm not sure if he's ever set foot in my office. My heart is in some lower register. Let's just say Scrappy and I have never been on good terms. I first met him in the summer of 1984. I was newly ordained at Dolores Mission. He was fifteen years old, and his probation officer assigned him to the church to complete his hours of community service. The chip located on his shoulder was the size of a Pontiac. "I don't have to listen to you." "I don't have to do what you say."

Some five years later, I am standing in front of a packed church, preaching at the funeral of one of Scrappy's homeboys. "If you love Cuko and want to honor his memory," I say to the congregation, "then you will work for peace and love your enemies." Immediately, Scrappy stands up and moves out of his pew and into the center aisle. All eyes are on him. I stop speaking. The eternal scowl I had come to know in that summer of 1984 is fixed on me as he walks straight ahead. We stand face-to-face, he mad-dogs me with some intensity, then turns and exits the church by the side door.

Three years later, I'm riding my bike, as I would in those days, "patrolling" the projects at night. I enter Scrappy's barrio, and there is a commotion. The homies have formed a circle and clearly two of their rank are "goin' head up." I break through the mob and, indeed, find Scrappy throwing down with one of his own homies. I discover later that the beef was over some *jaina* (girl). I stop the fight, and Scrappy reaches into the front waist of his pants and pulls out a gun that he waves around wildly. The crowd seems to be more horrified than I am. There are great gasps and pleas,

"Hey, dog, damn, put the gun away."

"Don't disrespect G."

Scrappy steadies the gun right at me and grunts a half laugh, "Shiiittt, I'll shoot his ass too."

Are you getting a sense of what our relationship was like?

So years later when I see him enter my office, it takes me a moment, but I locate my heart, hiding in Filene's basement, and Marcos intercoms me: "Scrappy's here." Then his voice gets squeaky and tentative. "Ya wanna see him?" Marcos knew enough that this would be in some doubt. "'Course, send him in."

Scrappy is not a large fellow, but there is no fat in his midsize build. His hair is slicked back and his moustache is understated. He hugs me only because not to would be too awkward. We have, after all, known each other for twenty years.

He sits and wastes no time.

"Look, let's just be honest with each other and talk man to man. You know that I've never disrespected you."

I figure, why not, I'm gonna go for it.

"Well, how 'bout the time you walked out on my homily at Cuko's funeral? . . . or the time you pulled a *cuete* out on me?"

Scrappy looks genuinely perplexed by what I've just said and cocks and scrunches his face like a confused beagle.

"Yeah, well . . . besides that," he says.

Then we do something we never have in our two decades of knowing each other. We laugh. But really, truly laugh—head-resting-on-my-desk laughter. We carry on until this runs its course, and then Scrappy settles into the core of his being, beyond the bravado of his *chingón* status in his gang.

"I have spent the last twenty years building a reputation for myself . . . and now . . . I regret . . . that I even have one."

And then in another first, he cries. But really, truly cries. He is doubled over, and the rocking seems to soothe the release of this great ache. When the wailing stops and he comes up for air, he daubs his eyes and runs his sleeve across his nose. He finally makes eye contact.

"Now what do I do? I know how to sell drugs. I know how to gangbang. I know how to shank fools in prison. I don't know how to change the oil in my car. I know how to drive, but I don't know how to park. And I don't know how to wash my clothes except in the sink of a cell."

I hire him that day, and he begins work the next morning on our graffiti crew.

Scrappy discovered, as Scripture has it, "that where he is standing is holy ground." He found the narrow gate that leads to life. God's voice was not of restriction, to "shape up or ship out." Scrappy found himself in the center of vastness and right in the expansive heart of God. The sacred place toward which God had nudged Scrappy all his life is not to be arrived at, but discovered.

Scrappy did not knock on the door so God would notice him. No need for doors at all. Scrappy was already inside.

*   *   *

God seems to be an unwilling participant in our efforts to pigeonhole Him. The minute we think we've arrived at the most expansive sense of who God is, "this Great, Wild God," as the poet Hafez writes, breaks through the claustrophobia of our own articulation, and things get large again. Richard Rohr writes in *Everything Belongs* that nothing of our humanity is to be discarded. God's unwieldy love, which cannot be contained by our words, wants to accept all that we are and sees our humanity as the privileged place to encounter this magnanimous love. No part of our hardwiring or our messy selves is to be disparaged. Where we stand, in all our mistakes and imperfection, is holy ground. It is where God has chosen to be intimate with us and not in any way but this. Scrappy's moment of truth was not in recognizing what a disappointment he's been all these years. It came in realizing that God had been beholding him and smiling for all this time, unable to look anywhere else. It is certainly true that you can't judge a book by its cover, nor can you judge a book by its first chapter—even if that chapter is twenty years long. When the vastness of God meets the restriction of our own humanity, words can't hold it. The best we can do is find the moments that rhyme with this expansive heart of God.

Shortly after I was ordained, I spent a year in Cochabamba, Bolivia. It was a gracious time that changed me forever. My Spanish was quite poor, and the year was to be filled with language study and ministry. I could celebrate the Eucharist in Spanish (after a summer at Dolores Mission), but I was a slave to the missal for some time to come. Early on, I began to minister to a community named Temporal, which had been without a priest for a long time. A few weeks into my time there, I was approached by a group of health workers who asked me to celebrate Mass in Tirani. This was a Quechua community located high above Cochabamba, whose indigenous folks harvested flowers for market. It was common to see campesinos making the long trek from Tirani with a huge weight of flowers tied to their backs. Like beasts of burden, they were doubled over all the way to town.

The health workers explain that the Quechua Indians in Tirani have not seen a priest in a decade, so they ask me to celebrate the Mass in Spanish, and one of the workers would preach in Quechua. (Everyone there speaks Quechua, with only the men able to defend themselves in Spanish.) The workers pick me up at the bottom of the hill at one o'clock on a Sunday afternoon. I hop into the back of the open-air truck with the others, and we climb to the top of the mountain. Midtrek, I decide to do an inventory of the contents of my backpack. I have brought everything I need *but* a missalette. I have not the *words*. At this point in my early priesthood, I couldn't wing Mass in English. The thought of doing so in Spanish was preposterous. I do have a Spanish Bible, so I frantically flip through the pages, trying to find any passages that sound like the words of consecration. "Take this and eat."

I locate any part of the New Testament that has Jesus kicking it at a table and eating. Soon, my body is introducing me to the marvels of flop sweat—and I haven't even arrived at Tirani yet. I am red in the face and stingy hot.

We pull into a huge, open-air landing, a field cleared of all crops, and many hundreds of Quechua Indians have gathered and set themselves down around this table, our altar. I hobble and fake my way through the liturgy of the Word, aided by the health workers, who read everything in Quechua. After the gentleman preaches, it is my turn to carry the ball. I'm like someone who's been in a major car accident. I can't remember a thing.

I know only that I have a crib sheet with some notes I have made, with stolen scriptural quotations, all the while lifting the bread and wine whenever I run out of things to say. It would be hard to imagine this Mass going worse.

When it is over, I am left spent and humiliated. I am wandering adrift, trying to gather my shattered self back together again, when a female health worker walks an ancient Quechua woman up to me.

"She hasn't gone to confession in ten years."

She leaves her with me, and the *viejita* unloads a decade's worth of sins in a singsongy and rapid-fire Quechua. I just nod like a *menso* waiting for a pause that might indicate she's finished. The woman's got some *pulmones* on her and doesn't seem to need to take a breath. She goes on for about a half hour. Finally she does stop, and I manage to communicate some penance and give her my memorized absolution. She walks away, and I turn to discover that I have been abandoned. The field where we celebrated Mass has been vacated. Inexplicably, even the truck and the health workers are gone. I am alone at the top of this mountain, stuck, not only without a ride, but in stultifying humiliation. I am convinced that a worse priest has never visited this place or walked this earth.

With my backpack snug on my shoulder and spirit deflated, I begin to make the long walk down the mountain and back to town. But before I leave the makeshift soccer field that had been our cathedral, an old Quechua campesino, seemingly out of nowhere, makes his way to me. He appears ancient, but I suspect his body has been weathered by work and the burden of an Indian's life. As he nears me, I see he is wearing tethered wool pants, with a white buttoned shirt, greatly frayed at the collar. He has a rope for a belt. His suit coat is coarse and worn. He has a fedora, toughened by the years. He is wearing huaraches, and his feet are caked with Bolivian mud. Any place that a human face can have wrinkles and creases, he has them. He is at least a foot shorter than I am, and he stands right in front of me and says, *"Tatai."*

This is Quechua for *Padrecito,* a word packed with *cariño,* affection, and a charming intimacy. He looks up at me, with penetrating, weary eyes and says, *"Tatai, gracias por haber venido"* (Thanks for coming).

I think of something to say, but nothing comes to me. Which is just as well, because before I can speak, the old campesino reaches into the pockets of his suit coat and retrieves two fistfuls of multicolored rose petals. He's on the tips of his toes and gestures that I might assist with the inclination of my head. And so he drops the petals over my head, and I'm without words. He digs into his pockets again and manages two more fistfuls of petals. He does this again and again, and the store of red, pink, and yellow rose petals seems infinite. I just stand there and let him do this, staring at my own huaraches, now moistened with my tears, covered with rose petals. Finally, he takes his leave and I'm left there, alone, with only the bright aroma of roses.

For all the many times I would return to Tirani and see the same villagers, over and over, I never saw this old campesino again.

God, I guess, is more expansive than every image we think rhymes with God. How much greater is the God we have than the one we think we have. More than anything else, the truth of God seems to be about a joy that is a foreigner to disappointment and disapproval. This joy just doesn't know what we're talking about when we focus on the restriction of not measuring up. This joy, God's joy, is like a bunch of women lined up in the parish hall on your birthday, wanting only to dance with you—cheek to cheek. "First things, recognizably first," as Daniel Berrigan says. The God, who is greater than God, has only one thing on Her mind, and that is to drop, endlessly, rose petals on our heads. Behold the One who can't take His eyes off of you.

Marinate in the vastness of that.

2

Dis-Grace

Most of the Masses I do in the probation camps take place on Saturday morning. Then I race home for an afternoon of baptisms, weddings, and *quinceañeras* at Dolores Mission. These usually start at one or two in the afternoon. I have a narrow window of half an hour one day between my morning Masses in the camps and my one o'clock baptism, so I stop by the office and go through the day's mail. I'm not there fifteen minutes, when this woman in her thirties walks through the door. I immediately glance at the clock hanging on the wall. I check how much time I have left before the baptism and am already lamenting that I most probably won't get to all the mail.

I find out later that the woman's name is Carmen. She's a recognizable figure on First Street, and yet this is her first visit to Homeboy. Today is the moment she chooses. Carmen is a heroin addict, a gang member, street person, occasional prostitute, and a champion *peleonera*. She's often defiantly storming down the street, usually shouting at someone. She's a real *gritona*, hollering at the men inside the Mitla Bar as she stumbles out to the sidewalk. I've heard her a number of times, arguing loudly on the pay phone with relatives or friends, "Daaammmnnn, JUST LET ME STAY TONIGHT."

Now I have seven minutes until my baptism. Carmen is a dusty blond, which couldn't be the color God originally gave her. She's attractive but so worn, by heroin and street life. She plops herself into one of the chairs in my office and cuts the fat out of her introductory remarks.

"I need help," she launches right in, brash and something of a "no-shit-sister." "Ooooooohhh," she says, "I been ta like fifty rehabs. I'm known all over . . . nationwide."

She smiles. Her eyes wander around my office, and she studies all the photographs hanging there. She multitasks, and her inspection of the place doesn't derail her stream-of-consciousness rambling. The family will arrive for the baptism in five minutes.

"I went to Catholic school all my life. Fact, I graduated from high school even. Fact, right after graduation, is when I started to use heroin." Carmen enters some kind of trance at this point, and her speech slows to deliberate and halting.

"And I . . . have been trying to stop . . . since . . . the moment I began."

Then I watch as Carmen tilts her head back until it meets the wall. She stares at the ceiling, and in an instant her eyes become these two ponds, water rising to meet their edges, swollen banks, spilling over. Then, for the first time really, she looks at me, and straightens.

"I . . . am . . . a . . . disgrace."

Suddenly, her shame meets mine. For when Carmen walked through that door, I had mistaken her for an interruption.

Author John Bradshaw claims that shame is at the root of all addictions. This would certainly seem to be true with the gang addiction. In the face of all this, the call is to allow the painful shame of others to have a purchase on our lives. Not to fix the pain but to feel it. Beldon Lane, the theologian, writes: "Divine love is incessantly restless until it turns all woundedness into health, all deformity into beauty and all embarrassment into laughter."

Yet, there is a palpable sense of disgrace strapped like an oxygen tank onto the back of every homie I know. In a letter from prison, a gang member writes, "people see me like less." This is hard to get through and penetrate. "You're no good." "You live in the projects." "Your mom's a basehead." "Your dad's a *tecato*." "You're wearing the same clothes today that you wore yesterday."

I had a little project kid in my office, who, someone told me, had regularly been late for school and missing class. So I bring this to his attention.

"I hear you've been late for school a lot."

He cries immediately, "I don't got that much clothes."

He had so internalized the fact that he didn't have clean clothes (or enough of them) that it infected his very sense of self.

I knew an inmate, Lefty, at Folsom State Prison, whose father would, when Lefty was a child, get drunk and beat his mom. One Saturday night Lefty's father beat his mother so badly that the next day she had to be led around by his sisters, as if she were blind. Both of her eyes were swollen shut.

On Sunday, Lefty's father and brothers are sitting on the couch, watching a football game. Lefty calmly goes into his parents' bedroom, retrieves a gun from his father's bedstand, and walks out to the living room. Lefty places himself in front of the television. His father and brothers push themselves as far back into the couch as possible, horrified. Lefty points the gun at his father and says, "You are my father, and I love you. If you ever hit my mother again . . . I . . . will . . . kill you."

Lefty was nine years old. He didn't kill his father, then (or ever). And yet, part of the spirit dies a little each time it's asked to carry more than its weight in terror, violence, and betrayal. "By the tender mercy of God," Scripture has it, "the dawn from on high will break upon us to give light to those who sit in darkness and in the shadow of death to guide our feet in the way of peace." How do those who "sit in darkness" find the light?

The poet Shelley writes, "To love and bear, to hope till hope creates from its own wreck the thing it contemplates."

How does one hang in there with folks, patiently taking from the wreck of a lifetime of internalized shame, a sense that God finds them (us) wholly acceptable?

Part of the problem is that, at its core, we tend to think that shame and sin, if you will, happen to someone else. My shame can't meet Carmen's unless I dispel that notion. I remember a woman who came to Mass every day at Dolores Mission, and during the time of petitionary prayer she always said the same thing: "Por los pecadores, para que ELLOS . . ." (For sinners, so that THEY . . .) It was never "sinners, we." It seemed outside of who she was. Yet, it's precisely within the contour of one's shame that one is summoned to wholeness. "Even there, even there," Psalm 39 tells us—even in the darkest place, we are known—yes, even there. My own falsely self-assertive and harmful, unfree ego gets drawn into the expansive heart of God. It is precisely in the light of God's vastness and acceptance of me that I can accept the harm I do for what it is.

There is a longing in us all to be God-enthralled. So enthralled that to those hunkered down in their disgrace, in the shadow of death, we become transparent messengers of God's own tender mercy. We want to be seized by that same tenderness; we want to bear the largeness of God.

* * *

I hate the Fourth of July. In my barrio, it lasts two whole months. All of June and all of July. The place is Beirut for sixty days—fireworks, firecrackers, sticks of dynamite. Endless and annoying. On one Tuesday morning, during this season, I'm in my office, and suddenly there is the rat-a-tat-tat of successive firecrakers whose source seems to be the bathroom off the kitchen area. The din is astounding, and, of course, I'm madder'n hell. By the time I get there, a homegirl, Candy, is a banshee, screaming in the *máscara* of the alleged culprit, Danny.

"How dare you disrespect G's office like that?"

"Who are you to tell me something?" he roars back. At nineteen years old, he's a runt half Candy's size, but he's certainly not going to "let himself." I can smell the sulfur of the firecrackers wafting out of the bathroom as I peel these two apart and lead Danny out to the parking lot.

Normally, I'd want to throttle this kid and give him, as they say, "what for." I manage something I rarely can. I morph into Mother Teresa *and* Gandhi.

"How ya doin?" I gently speak to Danny, on the hot asphalt of the parking lot.

"I DIDN'T DID IT!" Danny gives me both barrels, in perfect homie grammar. "I DID'NT . . . DID IT!"

"I know," I say, in full *agere contra* mode, going against every grain in my being. "I know, I know. But I'm worried about ya," I say, as quiet as I can be. "How ya doin?"

"Okay."

"Did you eat anything today?"

"No."

I give him five dollars.

"Why don't you go across the street to Jim's and get something to eat."

Danny starts to walk away and mumbles loud enough to be heard, "Even though you don't believe me." I call him back.

"Danny, if you tell me you didn't do it, *mijo*, then . . . that's all I need." Danny stands in the hot July sun and begins to weep. Cornered by shame and disgrace, he acquiesces to a vastness not mine.

Author and psychiatrist James Gilligan writes that the self cannot survive without love, and the self, starved of love, dies. The absence of self-love is shame, "just as cold is the absence of warmth." Disgrace obscuring the sun.

Guilt, of course, is feeling bad about one's actions, but shame is feeling bad about oneself. Failure, embarrassment, weakness, overwhelming worthlessness, and feeling disgracefully "less than"—all permeating the marrow of the soul.

Mother Teresa told a roomful of lepers once how loved by God they were and a "gift to the rest of us." Interrupting her, an old leper raises his hand, and she calls on him. "Could you repeat that again? It did me good. So, would you mind . . . just saying it again."

Franciscan Richard Rohr writes that "the Lord comes to us disguised as ourselves."

We've come to believe that we grow into this. The only thing we know about Jesus "growing up" is that he "grew in age, wisdom and favor with God." But do we really grow in favor with God? Did Jesus become increasingly more favorable to God, or did he just discover, over time, that he was wholly favorable?

* * *

Lula grew up in our office. He's in his early twenties now and has a son. He was ten when he first wandered in. I'd met him in Aliso Village at the annual Easter egg hunt. This was no White House lawn affair, just something thrown together very last minute by the ladies of the parish, but the kids seemed to have a good time. Lula was a skinny kid, who looked straight out of the Third World, undernourished, filthy. He was standing by himself, and no one seemed to include him or pay him much attention, except when they'd steal his eggs.

"My name is Luis, but everybody calls me Lula," he said.

I remember this a week later, when I pull up to an intersection and see him entering the crosswalk alone, his walk clumsy and self-conscious. I roll down my window and catch his attention. "Hey, Lula."

You would have thought I had electrocuted him. His whole body spasms with delight to be known, to be called, to hear his name uttered out loud. For his entire trip through the crosswalk, Lula kept turning back and looking at me, smiling.

Lula didn't do well in school. He was "special ed" throughout and famously a slowpoke. It was often the third bounce before he got what you were talking about. He didn't know how to tell time until Lupe Mosqueda, a member of our staff, taught him using a paper plate with movable hands. He was probably fifteen when he learned the concept of time.

All of us at Homeboy taught him to remember his birthday. Until he was fourteen, he had no clue. Once he walked into the office wearing one of those red ribbons given at school to commemorate one thing or another.

"Hey, Lula," I ask him, "What's the ribbon for?"

He stares intently at it and thinks for a goodly amount of time.

"FOR FREE DRUGS," he says.

"Well, Lula," I help, "maybe it stands for . . . Drug-Free Week?"

"Yeah," he says, "Dat one."

When he was seventeen, he was included in a youth group trip to Washington, D.C. Someone subsidized his trip. While there, he finds a pay phone on the Mall and calls the Homeboy toll-free number.

"I'M CALLIN' FROM THE MEMORIAL," he shouts.

"WHICH MEMORIAL, LULA?" I shout back, over the din of his background noise.

Lula pauses a really long time, because, I suspect, he doesn't actually know.

"THE PENNY GUY," he shouts.

"You mean the Lincoln Memorial?" I say.

"YEAH," he concedes, "DAT ONE."

When Lula first started to come to the office, shortly after I met him, he'd make a beeline to my office and just sit there. He was not much of a conversationalist.

One day, when Lula passed by all the other desks and staff members to get to my office, several called him back. "Lula, you come back here." "Hey, where do you think you're going?" They proceeded to explain to Lula the whole "what are we, chopped liver?" concept, that it was rude to walk past folks without greeting them. They suggested he try it again. Lula goes to the front door, exuberant at the mere idea that folks would actually want to be greeted by him. He walks in again and in a singsongy, lilting voice, nearly approximating Gregorian Chant says, "HELL-LOOOO, EVERYYYYBOOODDY!"

He would enter our office for the next five years with this exact same greeting.

Lula came from a huge family, and he was attention deficient, except in our office. Everyone lavished Lula with care he didn't get otherwise.

Ten-year-old Lula walks into my office one day and stands in the doorway. I suppose he's kept from fully entering by the fact that we are in the midst of a meeting with the job developers. He's positioned at the entrance and holds up a piece of paper, smiling broadly and doing a dance not unlike one that indicates the need for a restroom. I can see from where I sit that it's a report card. That Lula, who does so poorly in school, would be ecstatic about his grades, is cause to halt the meeting.

"You come on over here, Lula." I wave him in, and he navigates the adults who are sitting in his way. He hands me the report card and stands by my side, resting his elbow on my shoulder. His glee cannot be contained. I glance across the piece of paper in front of me and locate the subjects. F, F, F, F, F, F. All Fs and nothing but damn Fs. I think, *Why's he so excited to show me this thing?* I am frantically perusing every inch of this report card to find something, anything, for which to praise Lula. I find it.

Absences: 0.

"Lula, nice goin', *mijo*, you didn't miss a day (I'm thinking, *a lot a good it did ya*)—you didn't miss a day."

I high-five him as he starts to leave the office.

One of our job developers, John Tostado, stops Lula right there.

"Hey, Lula, how would you like to win five dollars?"

Lula indicates that he'd like this just fine.

"So here's the deal," John says, as he removes a crisp, new five-dollar bill from his wallet. "If you can answer this question correctly, the five dollars are yours."

Lula starts to giggle, and you can practically see him readying for battle. He actually limbers up and shakes himself out. For Lula, this is the College Bowl.

"All right, Lula, here's the question," John begins, his voice the moral equivalent of a drum roll.

"How . . . old . . . was . . . I . . . when I was . . . your age?"

Lula contorts his face and pounds his small fist against his forehead, herniating himself to come up with the right answer. All of us in the room hold our collective breath. A moment comes when you actually can see the light bulb above Lula's head ding "on."

"TEN YEARS OLD," Lula belts out.

High fives abound, and Lula is handed his cash prize. He walks to the door and holds up the booty with his two hands.

"That was easy," he says.

Simone Weil was right: "Those who are unhappy have no need for anything in this world, but people capable of giving them their attention."

You could add to that, the need to pull the "favor" right out of you, so that you don't try to grow in favor but recognize that you have always been wholly favorable.

Homies have been "outside" for so long they forget there is an inside. Their sense of isolation is suffocating, and they are quick to throw in the towel. One day, a very sad kid stumbles into my office and collapses into a chair. A homie with kids and other adult worries before he's able to handle them, he just gives up.

"That's it. I'm moving."

"Where ya movin' to?"

"Mars."

"Mars?"

"Yeah. This planet is tired of my ass already."

A homie trying to put words to this particular pain writes, "My spirit is so sore. It hurts to be me."

On occasion, I will do an intake on a homie who comes into our office looking for one of our services: tattoo removal, job placement, counseling, etc. If I had a dollar for every time the following happens, I could close down my development office.

I have the intake form, and I'm interviewing the homie seated in front of me. "How old are you?"

And the homie says, "Me?"

And I'm thinking, *No, what's your dog's age?* We are the only ones in the room, and he says, "Me?"

"Well, yes, you."

"Oh, I'm eighteen."

"Do you have a driver's license?"

"Me?"

(Again, I think, *No, I was wondering if your grandmother is still driving.*)

"Yes, you."

"No, I don't have a license."

The toxicity gets so internalized that it obliterates the "me." You couldn't possibly have interest in knowing things about "me." Sure you're not talking about somebody else—who happens not to be in the room?

All throughout Scripture and history, the principal suffering of the poor is not that they can't pay their rent on time or that they are three dollars short of a package of Pampers.

As Jesus scholar Marcus Borg points out, the principal suffering of the poor is shame and disgrace. It is a toxic shame—a global sense of failure of the whole self. This shame can seep so deep down. I asked a homie once, after Mass at a probation camp, if he had any brothers and sisters.

"Yeah," he says, "I have one brother and one sister," and then he's quick to add, with emphasis, "but THEY'RE GOOD."

"Oh," I tell him, "and that would make YOU . . . ?"

"Here," he says, "locked up."

"And THAT would make you . . . ?" I try again.

"Bad," he says.

Homies seem to live in the zip code of the eternally disappointing, and need a change of address. To this end, one hopes (against all human inclination) to model not the "one false move" God but the "no matter whatness" of God. You seek to imitate the kind of God you believe in, where disappointment is, well, Greek to Him. You strive to live the black spiritual that says, "God looks beyond our fault and sees our need."

Before this can take hold in gang members, they strut around in protective shells of posturing, which stunts their real and complete selves.

Dis-Grace

*   *   *

Often after Mass at the camps, kids will line up to talk one-on-one. The volunteers sometimes invite the minors to confession, but usually the kids just want to talk, be heard, get a blessing. At Camp Afflerbaugh, I'm seated on a bench outside in a baseball field, and one by one, the homies come over to talk briefly. This day, there's quite a lineup. The next kid approaching, I can tell, is all swagger and pose. His walk is *chingon* in its highest gear. His head bobs, side-to-side, to make sure all eyes are riveted. He sits down, we shake hands, but he seems unable to shake the scowl etched across his face.

"What's your name? I ask him.

"SNIPER," he sneers.

"Okay, look (I had been down this block before), I have a feeling you didn't pop outta your mom and she took one look at your ass and said, 'Sniper.' So, come on, dog, what's your name?"

"Gonzalez," he relents a little.

"Okay now, son, I know the staff here will call you by your last name. I'm not down with that. Tell me, *mijo*, what's your mom call you?"

"Cabrón."

There is even the slightest flicker of innocence in his answer.

"*Oye, no cabe duda.* But, son, I'm looking for birth certificate here."

The kid softens. I can tell it's happening. But there is embarrassment and a newfound vulnerability.

"*Napoleón,*" he manages to squeak out, pronouncing it in Spanish.

"Wow," I say, "That's a fine, noble, historic name. But I'm

almost positive that when your *jefita* calls you, she doesn't use the whole nine *yardas*. Come on, *mijito*, do you have an *apodo*? What's your mom call you?"

Then I watch him go to some far, distant place—a location he has not visited in some time. His voice, body language, and whole being are taking on a new shape—right before my eyes.

"Sometimes,"—his voice so quiet, I lean in—"sometimes . . . when my mom's not mad at me . . . she calls me . . . Napito."

I watched this kid move, transformed, from Sniper to Gonzalez to Cabrón to Napoleón to Napito. We all just want to be called by the name our mom uses when she's not pissed off at us.

Names are important. After all, the main occupation of most gang members most of the time is the writing of their *names* on walls. I recall on my first day of teaching at Loyola High School in Los Angeles in 1979, I was scared poopless about the prospect. With my arms filled with books, juggling the necessary cup of coffee, I walk to my first class. I stop in the doorway of a veteran teacher, Donna Wanland. She's at her desk, reading the morning *Times*.

"It's my first day of teaching," I say to her, "Give me some advice."

She doesn't turn from her paper but holds out her right hand, displaying two fingers.

"Two things," she says, "One: know all their names by tomorrow. Two: It's more important that they know you than that they know what ya know."

Good advice. I followed it and I think it served me in good stead. I remembered it when I arrived at Dolores Mission. Once I had made the decision to not be a slave to my office, I wandered the projects, often approaching (uninvited) the various groupings of gang members, which spotted every corner and crevice of the housing developments. The reception was almost always chilly. (This changed only after I began to visit homies from the community who were locked up or wounded in the hospital.)

There was one kid in particular everyone knew as Cricket. To say that he would "give me the cold shoulder" would impugn shoulders. Cricket, fifteen years old, would walk away when I approached and would return to the *bola* (I noticed) once I left. I investigated and discovered his name was William.

One day I walk up to this group of gang members, with Cricket among them, and he doesn't disappear on me. I shake hands with all of them, and when I get to Cricket, he actually lets me shake his hand.

"William," I say to him, "How you doin'? It's good to see ya."

William says nothing. But as I walk away (I always made a point of not staying very long), I can hear William in a very breathy, age-appropriate voice, say to the others, "Hey, the priest knows my name."

"I have called you by your name. You are mine," is how Isaiah gets God to articulate this truth. Who doesn't want to be called by name, known? The "knowing" and the "naming" seem to get at what Anne Lamott calls our "inner sense of disfigurement."

As misshapen as we feel ourselves to be, attention from another reminds us of our true shape in God.

I give credit for most of my gray hairs to a kid named Speedy. He was a thrill seeker in the world of project gangbanging. And I don't mean that in a good way. He was Evel Knievel, pulling off near-death-defying stunts—creeping into enemy territory, just so that he could, as it were, stick his thumbs in his ears, loll his tongue, and say "neener neener neener" at a *bola* of *vatos* that hated him in a big way. More than a few times, I'd see him attempt one of these "stick your head in the lion's mouth" moments, and I'd "chase his ass" back to his barrio, screaming at him, red-faced, saying things my mother never taught me. "Are you fucking out of your mind? Do you *want* to get killed?"

One afternoon I am in the sacristy at Dolores Mission, and per usual I'm late for the 5 p.m. Mass. My glances out to the body of the church catch *viejitas* looking at their watches, shrugging at one another. I'm vesting as fast as I can. Speedy enters the side door. He's a lanky guy at seventeen, rail thin but taut from, no doubt, being pursued by enemies all the time. He slides his two elbows on the Formica countertop and perches his chin on his fists. I'm flipping through books to find the readings.

"You know, G," he begins, "I don't really care if I live or die."

I'm embarrassed to admit, all I'm thinking of are the three old ladies who've been waiting for twenty minutes for *la misa* to start.

"Look, dog," I tell him, throwing a Guatemalan stole over my head, "I have to do Mass right now. It's gonna have to do for the moment, for you to know, that I care whether you live or die."

Speedy weighs this on some internal scale and things balance.

"Okay," he says, and I think the equivalent of *Whew*.

Three hours later, I'm sitting at my desk. In my pastor days, I kept the front door of the parish office open—giving you a clear shot of my inner office and my desk. Speedy appears, and his mood seems elevated; he dives right in.

"Look, I don't want you to get red at what I'm about to tell you."

This, of course, begins the reddening process for me.

"Whad ya do?" I ask, as he stands at the side of my desk, ready to rabbit jump out of my office if my red face turns explosive.

"Well . . . I walked Karla home."

Red face at morning, sailor take warning. I'm pissed. Karla is a very cute homegirl that Speedy is currently "sprung on," and she lives in the midst of Speedy's worst enemies. To walk her home was to endanger both their lives. It was unconscionable and irresponsible, and my face was flammable.

I don't get a chance to put words to my displeasure, because Speedy rapid-fires the rest of the story to me. He deposits Karla in her second-story apartment, and as he is descending the stairs, he encounters eight members of the dreaded rival gang. They aren't displeased to see him. They're salivating.

They chase him and throw whatever they can at him—rocks, sticks, empty bottles of 40 ouncers. (Had this story happened five years later, they would have had guns.) He eludes them, leaving them in the project dust. They don't call him Speedy for nothing.

As he nears First Street and can see the relative safety of his barrio across the street, he bumps into Yolanda, a woman active in the parish. She knows enough to know that Speedy should not be where he currently is. She summons him.

"*Ven, mijo. Qué estás haciendo aqui?*"

Speedy, out of breath and panting, lowers his head.

"*Sabes qué, mijo,*" she says, "*Te digo una cosa.* If anything happened to you, it would break my heart in two." She barely knows him. "You know I've seen you playing with your nephew in the park. What a good *tio* you are. I've also seen you feed the homeless at the church. What a generous and good thing that is."

Then she returns to her earlier refrain, with even more resolve soaked in it.

"*Pero, te digo una cosa*, if anything happened to you, it would break my heart in two. Now, *vete a la casa.*"

Speedy arrives at my office, out of breath from this encounter with a nearly perfect stranger.

He looks at me and smiles after the telling of his tale.

"You know," he says, tapping his heart with his finger, "that shit made me feel good."

Of course, it did. But what could be tinier in the scope of human relations than the tender mercy of this stranger, rubbing salve on the wounds of this kid's hopeless heart? You can almost hear the armor fall away and clank to the ground.

Not long after this, things started to change for Speedy—largely because he wanted them to. As Richard Rohr would say, he had decided to "live his way into a new way of thinking."

He married his, if not childhood sweetheart, his teenage one, Claudia. They moved away from the projects, and Speedy began work in an oil refinery in Richmond, California. They began a family and now have three kids, an older daughter and two boys. When Claudia had her first child, it was the summer of the movie *Free Willy.* And since she was so tiny and preposterously pregnant, "Willy" became my nickname for her. I called her on her birthday once.

"Happy Birthday, Willy," I tell her when she answers the phone.

"G, you remembered."

"So," I ask her, "What's your *ruco* got planned for you tonight?"

"Oh." She gets quiet. "You know, money's tight . . . and, well . . . we're just gonna stay home tonight."

"WHAT?! *No me digas,*" choosing to exaggerate wildly. *"Oye,* put that cheap *codo* on the phone."

Speedy steps up to the receiver.

"I can't believe you, dog," I start in on him, "I mean you can't squirrel away twenty bones to just take her out and eat, by candlelight, *tú sabes,* whispering in her ear, *'mi vida, mi reina, mi cielo, mi todo? Qué gacho,* right there.'"

Speedy thinks for half a beat.

"Damn," he says, "I bought her ass roses, what more she want?"

I can visualize Claudia, laughing and hugging "her man." The two of them, falling into each other's arms, holding on against the darkness and witnessing together, real light, real peace.

Speedy hailed from a family broken in all the usual ways. As a kid, he had to navigate alcoholism, fighting, estrangement, and inappropriateness on top of dysfunction stacked high onto sadness. As he's built a life for his own family, he's negotiated the landmines that were regularly detonated during his childhood.

One day he's in town and invites me to dinner. "I'll even pay," he says.

At the restaurant, we talk about his job, his return to school, his greater responsibility, and his newfound leadership role at the oil refinery. I ask about down time and what he does on Sunday.

"Well,"—he's ready to go into detail—"we begin with Mass. Then we head off to Mimi's Café. The kids can order whatever they want. We always go there. Then, we go to Barnes and Noble. Every Sunday, for two hours. Now, you know my cheap ass is not gonna buy any books. No, everyone picks out a book, and we all go to our separate corners. They be havin' comfortable chairs at Barnes and Noble. Then, when time's up, we put the books back. We don't sweat it. We'll be back next Sunday—pick up right where we left off."

I laugh and am both charmed and astonished.

"You know, the kids did beg me to buy the new Harry Potter book," he continues, "so, what the hell, I broke down and bought it. Now, you know what we do every night? I sit in my recliner. We turn off the TV. And my three kids read *Harry Potter*, out loud. First, my oldest, my daughter, she reads a whole page. Then she hands it to my son, and he reads a paragraph. Then the baby, with help from the other two, reads a sentence—but barely. And it gets passed back, you know, page, paragraph, sentence. And I," he starts to buckle and his voice trembles, "I . . . just close my eyes, sitting in my recliner . . . listening to my kids . . . read . . . out loud."

Speedy puts his hand up to his eyes, tearful, and is as surprised as I am where this story has taken him. I reach over, beyond his plate of a half-eaten steak, and grab his arm.

"You've got a good life," I tell him. The tears arrive now in their fullness, unencumbered and welcome, even.

"Yeah,"—he looks at me—"yeah . . . I do."

Out of the wreck of our disfigured, misshapen selves, so darkened by shame and disgrace, indeed the Lord comes to us disguised as ourselves. And we don't grow into this—we just learn to pay better attention. The "no matter whatness" of God dissolves the toxicity of shame and fills us with tender mercy. Favorable, finally, and called by name—by the one your mom uses when she's not pissed off.

3

Compassion

In 1993, I taught a course at Folsom Prison. "Theological Issues in American Short Fiction." From the beginning, the inmates said they wanted me to teach them something. Just not Scripture. I mentioned that I had an MA in English.

"Well, yeah, teach us that," they said.

So we would sit around in the chapel, some fifteen lifers and myself, and discuss short stories. I ended up teaching three classes of this short-story course on all three yards. (As in most prisons in California, they have three yards: A [special-needs yard or protective custody]; B [a tough and generally wild yard]; and C [a moderately "programming" yet very high security yard].) I settled on short stories so I could Xerox copies of really short ones and we'd read them out loud and discuss them.

One of the stories was Flannery O'Connor's "A Good Man Is Hard to Find." After they read it, we come to the Grandmother's transformation of character ("she would of been a good woman . . . if it had been somebody there to shoot her every minute of her life"). My students speak of this woman's change and seem to use these terms interchangeably: sympathy, empathy, and compassion. Like any teacher stalling until the bell rings, I ask these felons to define their terms.

"Well, sympathy," one begins, "is when your homie's mom dies and you go up to him and say, *''Spensa*—sorry to hear 'bout your moms.'"

Just as quickly, there is a volunteer to define empathy.

"Yeah, well, empathy is when your homie's mom dies and you say, *''Spensa,* 'bout your moms. *Sabes qué,* my moms died six months ago. I feel ya, dog.'"

"Excellent," I say. "Now, what's compassion?"

No takers.

The class collectively squirms and stares at their state-issue boots.

"Come on now," I say, "Compassion—what's it mean?"

Their silence is quite sustained, like visitors entering for the first time some sacred, mysterious temple.

Finally, an old-timer, down twenty-five years, tentatively raises his finger. I call on him.

"Well, now," he says, all eyes on him, shaking his head, "Compassion—that's sumthin' altogether different."

He ponders what he'll say next.

"Cause," he adds humbly, "That's what Jesus did. I mean, Compassion . . . IS . . . God."

God is compassionate, loving kindness. All we're asked to do is to be in the world who God is. Certainly compassion was the wallpaper of Jesus' soul, the contour of his heart, it was who he was. I heard someone say once, "Just assume the answer to every question is compassion."

Compassion

Jesus pulled this off. Compassion is no fleeting occasional emotion rising to the surface like eros or anger. It's full-throttled. Scripture scholars connect the word to the entrails, to the bowels, from the deepest part of the person. This was how Jesus was moved, from the entirety of his being. He was "moved with pity" when he saw folks who seemed like "sheep without a shepherd." He had room for everybody in his compassion.

In the earliest days of our storefront office, along with thousands of gang members from some forty gangs in the neighborhoods of the Hollenbeck Police Division, we'd be visited by countless kids making their way home to the projects from school. I had known all these kids and their families during my years as pastor, so they'd drop by from Second Street School and Hollenbeck Middle School. They'd just sit on the couch in the waiting area or play video games on the computers. They were dry, emaciated sponges hoping to catch a drop of adult attention. All of the staff got into the habit of asking each kid, daily, "So, what did you learn today that you never knew before?"

They got to dreading this question, because it forced them to think. "Buffalo—I learned about da buffalo."

"Fractions."

One junior high kid said, "I learned not to pick on girls."

"Oh, yeah, how'd you learn that?"

"I got slapped." (That'll do it.)

Errands were an almost daily occurrence. Someone on my staff would go to Office Depot or Smart & Final to pick up supplies, and the project kids would race to the staff member's car. The luckiest one would get to ride shotgun.

One day a tiny kid, twelve-year-old Betito, rests his head on his fists on the front of my desk. He looks forlorn and asks sadly, "Hey, G, are ya goin' anywhere?"

"No, *mijo*," I say.

He comes alive, "Can I go wit ya?"

The destination, apparently, was less important—it's the "going with" that counted.

Betito is a funny kid, bright and energetic, who comes alive when he steps into our office on First Street. He becomes a fixture there, and you can count on him arriving after school, greeting each one of my staff at their desks as he works the room. English is not his first language, and though all of us speak Spanish, Betito challenges himself in this, insisting on "English only." Betito is always picking up English expressions he hears on TV. He walks in one day, armed with some idiomatic argot courtesy of a Pollo Loco commercial.

"Hey, G, you know what you are?" his accent thick and halting. "You da real deal."

At a dollar ninety-nine.

Routines get born this way. Betito and I would try to catch each other. "Hey, Beto—you know why she said that about you?"

"No, why?"

"Cuz you're da real deal."

We both try to make the answer to every question, "the real deal." This even becomes our nicknames for each other, "*Oye, qué 'onda*, Real Deal?"

Betito is precocious for his age. He walks into my office one day, and stands in front of my desk, "Hey, G, kick me down wit twenty bones, yeah?"

I'm taken aback by his straight-out-there boldness.

"So what do you need twenty dollars for?"

64

"Takin' my lady to the movies."

"YOUR LADY?" I say to him, not feigning shock. "How old are you?"

"Twelve."

"TWELVE?" How old's your lady?"

"Sixteen."

"SIXTEEN?"

"Yeah," he says, calming me down with the flick of his hand, "but she's short."

(Oh . . . here's your twenty dollars, then).

One Sunday evening, Betito is playing with his cousin in Aliso Village. There is no school the next day—some Monday President's holiday or something. There are two gang members standing in front of a nearby dumpster, smoking *frajos*. A van pulls into the projects, with two gang members in the front seat. When they see the two smoking cigarettes in front of the dumpster, they open up fire. A bullet catches one of them. He drops. Everyone runs. Every man, woman, and child knows that when gunfire begins, you run, you duck, you hunker down behind some car or slink in between buildings. You move. Betito knows this. For some reason, though, he freezes there. And because he hesitates to seek cover, a very large bullet enters his side, above the waist, travels through, and exits the other side. They call these "through and throughs."

The doctor, a friend of mine, who would treat Betito, told me a week later that this bullet was the highest caliber he had ever seen. The sheer reverberation of the bullet traversing Betito's body rendered him paralyzed from the waist down. And the bullet hadn't even touched his spine.

Word gets to me, and I go straight to the hospital. Betito's grandmother and I keep vigil through the night, while the surgeons operate for some six hours. You don't really keep vigil; it keeps you—suspended in awkward silence and dead air—desperate for anything at all to stir some hope out of these murky waters and make things vital again.

Betito survives. But two hours into his recovery, I watch through the window of his room in intensive care as a team of nurses and doctors rush in and surround him. They pound on his chest. They beg and plead with his heart to cooperate. His heart finally deafens to their entreaties, and he dies.

Betito was precocious, funny, bold, and only twelve years old. He was the Real Deal.

If we long to be in the world who God is, then, somehow, our compassion has to find its way to vastness. It would rather not rest on the two in the van, aiming frighteningly large-caliber weaponry. I sure didn't. When they were caught and I found I knew them, it was excruciating not to be able to hate them. Sheep without a shepherd. And no less the real deal. But for lack of someone to reveal the truth to them, they had evaded healing, and the task of returning them to themselves got more hardened and difficult. But are they less worthy of compassion than Betito?

I will admit that the degree of difficulty here is exceedingly high. Kids I love killing kids I love. There is nothing neat in carving space for both in our compassion. I can recall a woman in the audience at a talk I gave in Orange County, rushing me during the question-and-answer period. She wanted to do me real harm. People had to restrain her and remove her from the audience. Her daughter had been set on fire by gang members. I represented to her the victimizers. It was a sobering moment, underscoring the precariousness of being too glib here. Sometimes it's enough simply to acknowledge how wide the gulf is that we all hope to bridge. But isn't the highest honing of compassion that which is hospitable to victim and victimizer both?

Dante speaks of having compassion for the damned. We need not feel ourselves as soft on crime if we see this kind of compassion as its highest calibration.

Jesus says if you love those who love you, big wow (which I believe is the original Greek). He doesn't suggest that we cease to love those who love us when he nudges us to love our enemies. Nor does Jesus think the harder thing is the better thing. He knows it's just the harder thing. But to love the enemy and to find some spaciousness for the victimizer, as well as the victim, resembles more the expansive compassion of God. That's why you do it.

To be in the world who God is.

Here is what we seek: a compassion that can stand in awe at what the poor have to carry rather than stand in judgment at how they carry it.

In the midnineties, I return to the office after a morning meeting to our storefront sandwiched between the Mitla Café and the furniture store. It's noonish. I stand in front of the desk of the receptionist, Michelle, who hands me my messages. As I sift through them, someone taps me on my left shoulder. It's Looney. He gives me a big *abrazote*.

"*Oye, mijo,*" I say, "when'd you get out?"

The smile is bigger than he is.

"*Ayer.*"

Looney is a fifteen-year-old from a gang located close to our office. He is a *chaparrito*, barely reaches my chest, and he has just been disgorged from one of the twenty-four probation camps in

Los Angeles County. His sentence was a mere six months, but it was his first such detention. Having been put on probation for writing on walls, his probation officer cited him for a violation when he stopped going to school and sent him away.

Emily, one of our office workers, sidles up to Michelle to cheerlead and add to the welcome, project-style.

Emily turns to Michelle and conspires.

"*Oye*, look at Looney . . . he's so ttttaaaaaallll." Her words seem to elbow Michelle in her side.

"Yeeeaaahhh," Michelle adds, "He's so bbbiiigggg."

"He's a maaaaaan already," Emily plants the finishing touch.

Looney is both loving this attention and thinking maybe six months more in camp would not be so bad.

Michelle and Emily have taken it upon themselves to kill the fatted pepperoni and welcome home the prodigal Looney. When five extremely large pizzas arrive, they hand me the bill, which I don't seem to recall from the gospel account.

We cram ourselves onto the tiny couch in the even sparser reception area and eat our pizza. All the office staff join in. Looney is luminous and giddy in his awkwardness, eyes darting to all of us gathered around, trying to measure our delight in his return. He can barely believe that it's so high.

I'm sitting on the arm of the couch, eating my slice, and Looney leans in to me, with a whisper, "Can I talk ta ya, G . . . alone . . . in your office?"

I gather my grub and sit behind my desk. He moves a chair, situated too far for his liking, and presses it very close to the front of my desk. He extricates a long envelope, squished in his side pocket, and proudly slaps it in front of me on my desk.

"My grades," he announces, "from camp."

His voice has moved to a preadolescent octave of excitement, and I scurry to join him at the parade.

"*De veeeras,*" as I relieve the transcript from its container.

Looney straightens his back and hops a little in the chair.

"Straight A's," he says.

"*Seeeerrrriioo?*" I say.

"*Me la rallo,*" he says. "Straight A's."

Like a kid fumbling with wrapping on a present, I get the transcript out and extend it open. And, sure enough, right there before my eyes: 2 Cs; 2 Bs; 1 A.

And I think, *Close enough.* Not the straightest A's I've ever seen. I decide not to tell Looney he's an "unreliable reporter" here.

"Wow, *mijo,*" I tell him, "*Bien hecho.* Nice goin'."

I carefully refold the transcript and put it back in the envelope.

"On everything I love, *mijo,*" I say to him, "if you were my son, I'd be the proudest man alive."

In a flash, Looney situates his thumb and first finger in his eye sockets, trembling, and wanting to stem the flow of tears, which seem to be inevitable at this point. Like the kid with the fingers in the dike, he's shaking now and desperate not to cry. I look at this little guy and know that he has been returned to a situation largely unchanged. Parents are either absent at any given time or plagued by mental illness. Chaos and dysfunction is what will now surround him as before. His grandmother, a good woman, whose task it is now to raise this kid, is not quite up to the task. I know that one month before this moment I buried Looney's best friend, killed in our streets for no reason at all. So I lead with my gut.

"I bet you're afraid to be out, aren't you?"

This seems to push the Play button on Looney's tear ducts,

and quickly he folds his arms on the front of my desk and rests his sobbing head on his folded arms. I let him cry it out. Finally, I reach across the desk and place my hand on his shoulder.

"You're gonna be okay."

Looney sits up with what is almost defiance and tends to the wiping of his tears.

"I . . . just . . . want . . . to have a life."

I am taken aback by the determination with which he says this.

"Well, *mijo*," I say to him, "who told you that you wouldn't have one? I mean, remember the letters you used to write to me from camp, telling me about all the gifts and goodness you discovered in yourself—stuff you didn't know was there. Look, dog, I know you think you're in a deep, dark hole, *pero la neta*, you're in a tunnel. It's in the nature of tunnels that if you just keep walking, the light's gonna show up. Trust me, I can see it—I'm taller than you are."

Looney sniffles and nods and seems to listen.

"You're gonna be just fine . . . after all," and I hand him back his grades, "Straight A's."

If you read Scripture scholar Marcus Borg and go to the index in search of "sinner," it'll say, "see outcast." This was a social grouping of people who felt wholly unacceptable. The world had deemed them disgraceful and shameful, and this toxic shame, as I have mentioned before, was brought inside and given a home in the outcast.

Jesus' strategy is a simple one: He eats with them. Precisely to those paralyzed in this toxic shame, Jesus says, "I will eat with you." He goes where love has not yet arrived, and he "gets his grub on." Eating with outcasts rendered them acceptable.

Pizzas all around—Looney's home.

Compassion

Recognizing that we are wholly acceptable is God's own truth for us—waiting to be discovered.

*   *   *

Pema Chödrön, an ordained Buddhist nun, writes of compassion and suggests that its truest measure lies not in our service of those on the margins, but in our willingness to see ourselves in kinship with them. In 1987 Dolores Mission Church declared itself a sanctuary church for the undocumented, after passage of the Immigration Reform and Control Act of 1986. Soon, recently arrived undocumented men from Mexico and Central America would sleep each night in the church (Guadalupe Homeless Project), and women and children, in the convent (Casa Miguel Pro).

Attention followed and lots of it. The media swarmed the place in these earliest days. As almost always happens, attention begets opposition. I used to dread clearing the parish's answering machine during this period. It always had a handful of hate messages and vague (and not so vague) death threats.

Once, while I turn the corner in front of the church, heading to a CEB meeting in the projects, I am startled by letters spray-painted crudely across the front steps:

WETBACK CHURCH

The chill of it momentarily stops me. In an instant, you begin to doubt and question the price of things. I acknowledge how much better everything is when there is no cost and how I prefer being hoisted on shoulders in acclaim to the disdain of anonymous spray cans.

I arrive at the meeting and tell the gathered women about our hostile visitor during the night.

"I guess I'll get one of the homies to clean it up later."

Petra Saldana, a normally quiet member of the group, takes charge.

"You will not clean that up."

Now, I was new at the parish and my Spanish was spotty. I understood the words she spoke but had difficulty circling in on the sense of it.

"You will not clean this up. If there are people in our community who are disparaged and hated and left out because they are *mojados* (wetbacks) . . ." Then she poises herself on the edge of the couch, practically ready to leap to her feet. "Then we shall be proud to call ourselves a wetback church."

These women didn't just want to serve the less fortunate, they were anchored in some profound oneness with them and became them.

"That you may be one as the Father and I are one."

Jesus and Petra are on the same page here. They chose a oneness in kinship and a willingness to live in others' hearts. Jesus was not a man *for* others. He was one *with* others. There is a world of difference in that. Jesus didn't seek the rights of lepers. He *touched* the leper even before he got around to curing him. He didn't champion the cause of the outcast. He *was* the outcast. He didn't fight for improved conditions for the prisoner. He simply said, "I was in prison."

The strategy of Jesus is not centered in taking the right stand on issues, but rather in standing in the right place—with the outcast and those relegated to the margins.

Once the homeless began to sleep in the church at night, there was always the faintest evidence that they had. Come Sunday morning, we'd foo foo the place as best we could. We would sprinkle I Love My Carpet on the rugs and vacuum like crazy. We'd strategically place potpourri and Air Wick around the church to combat this lingering, pervasive reminder that nearly fifty (and later up to one hundred) men had spent the night there. About the only time we used incense at Dolores Mission was on Sunday morning, before the 7:30 a.m. Mass crowd would arrive. Still, try as we might, the smell remained. The grumbling set in, and people spoke of "churching" elsewhere.

It was at about this time that a man drove by the church and stopped to talk to me. He was Latino, in a nice car, and had arrived at some comfortable life and living. He knew I was the pastor. He waxed nostalgic about having grown up in the projects and pointed to the church and said he had been baptized and made his first communion there.

Then he takes in the scene all around him. Gang members gathered by the bell tower, homeless men and women being fed in great numbers in the parking lot. Folks arriving for the AA and NA meetings and the ESL classes.

It's a Who's Who of Everybody Who Was Nobody. Gang member, drug addict, homeless, undocumented. This man sees all this and shakes his head, determined and disgusted, as if to say "tsk tsk."

"You know," he says, "This *used* to be a church."

I mount my high horse and say, "You know, most people around here think it's *finally* a church."

Then I ride off into the sunset.

Roll credits.

The smell was never overwhelming, just undeniably there. The Jesuits figured that if "we can't fix it, then we'll feature it." So we determined to address the discontent in our homilies one

Sunday. Homilies were often dialogic in those days, so one day I begin with, "What's the church smell like?"

People are mortified, eye contact ceases, women are searching inside their purses for they know not what.

"Come on, now," I throw back at them, "what's the church smell like?"

"*Huele a patas*" (Smells like feet), Don Rafael booms out. He was old and never cared what people thought.

"Excellent. But why does it smell like feet?"

"Cuz many homeless men slept here last night?" says a woman.

"Well, why do we let that happen here?"

"*Es nuestro compromiso*" (It's what we've committed to do), says another.

"Well, why would anyone commit to do that?"

"*Porque es lo que haria Jesús.*" (It what's Jesus would do.)

"Well, then . . . what's the church smell like now?"

A man stands and bellows, "*Huele a nuestro compromiso*" (it smells like commitment).

The place cheers.

Guadalupe waves her arms wildly, "*Huele a rosas*" (smells like roses).

The packed church roars with laughter and a newfound kinship that embraced someone else's odor as their own. The stink in the church hadn't changed, only how the folks saw it. The people at Dolores Mission had come to embody Wendell Berry's injunction: "You have to be able to imagine lives that are not yours."

Scripture scholars contend that the original language of the Beatitudes should not be rendered as "Blessed are the singlehearted" or "Blessed are the peacemakers" or "Blessed are those who struggle for justice." Greater precision in translation would say, "You're in the right place if . . . you are single-hearted or work for peace." The Beatitudes is not a spirituality, after all. It's a geography. It tells us where to stand.

Compassion isn't just about feeling the pain of others; it's about bringing them in toward yourself. If we love what God loves, then, in compassion, margins get erased. "Be compassionate as God is compassionate," means the dismantling of barriers that exclude.

In Scripture, Jesus is in a house so packed that no one can come through the door anymore. So the people open the roof and lower this paralytic down through it, so Jesus can heal him. The focus of the story is, understandably, the healing of the paralytic. But there is something more significant than that happening here. They're ripping the roof off the place, and those outside are being let in.

* * *

I met Anthony through legendary Eastside probation officer Mary Ridgway. "Help this kid," she pleads over the phone.

Mary told me where I might bump into him, since his last known address was his car, left for dead on Michigan Street.

At nineteen years old, Anthony had been on his own for a while. His parents had disappeared long ago in a maelstrom of heroin and prison time, and he was fending for himself, selling the occasional vial of PCP to buy Big Macs and the occasional Pastrami Madness at Jim's. He was a tiny fella, and when he spoke, his voice was puny, reed-thin, and high-pitched. If you closed your eyes, you'd think you were "conversating" (as the homies say) with a twelve-year-old.

One day we're both leaning up against his "tore up" *ranfla*, and our conversation is drifting toward the "what do you want to be when you grow up" theme.

"I want to be a mechanic. Don't know nothing 'bout cars, really. But I'd like to learn it."

My mechanic, Dennis, on Brooklyn Avenue, was something of a legend in the barrio.

Dennis could fix any car. A tall, pole-thin, Japanese American in his near sixties, Dennis was a chain smoker. He was not a man of few words—he was a man of no damn words at all. He just smoked. You'd bring your car in, complaining of some noise under the hood, and hand the keys to Dennis, who would stand there with a cigarette dangling from his lips.

He'd take the keys, and when you returned the next day, he'd give you your car, purring as it should. No words were exchanged during this entire transaction.

So I go to Dennis to plead my case.

"Look, Dennis," I say, sitting in his cramped office, truly a smoke-filled room. "Hire this kid Anthony. True enough he doesn't know anything about cars, but he sure is eager, and I think he could learn stuff."

Dennis just stares at me, nodding slightly, a long ash hovering at the end of his *frajo*, deciding whether to jump off the cliff or not. I redouble my efforts. I tell Dennis that this won't just be one job for one homie but will create a ripple effect of peace in the entire neighborhood. Long drags of silence and a stony stare. I get out my shovel and my top hat and cane. Nobel Peace Prize, will alter the course of history, will change the world as we know it. Nothing. Dennis just fills his lungs with smoke, as I fill the air with earnest pleas. Finally, I just give up and shut up. I've done the best I can and I'm ready to call it a day. Then Dennis takes one long last sucking drag on his cigarette and releases it into the air, smoke wafting in front of his face, clouding my view. Once every trace of smoke is let out, he looks at me, and this is the only thing he says that day:

"I will teach him everything I know."

And so Anthony became a mechanic. He would give me periodic updates.

"I learned how to do a lube job today."

"I fixed a carburetor all by myself."

He hands me a photograph one day. There is Anthony, with a broad smile, face smudged with axle grease, workshirt with ANTHONY embroidered proudly on his chest. No question, to look at this face is to know that its owner is a transformed man. But standing next to him in the picture, with an arm around Anthony (and a cigarette hanging out of his mouth) is Dennis, an equally changed human being. And all because Dennis, one day, decided to rip the roof off the place. Being in the world who God is. The ones on the outside have been let in.

Compassion is not a relationship between the healer and the wounded. It's a covenant between equals. Al Sharpton always says, "We're all created equal, but we don't all end up equal."

Compassion is always, at its most authentic, about a shift from the cramped world of self-preoccupation into a more expansive place of fellowship, of true kinship.

I take Julian and Matteo with me to give a talk in Helena, Montana. They both are "YA babies," having essentially grown up in Youth Authority facilities. Kids aren't meant to grow up there. From different gangs, and each at nineteen years old, they've missed a lot of life by being incarcerated the last four to five years. There is the usual panic, among homies, in flying. Two *viejitas* clinging arm in arm, blessing themselves incessantly, as the plane takes off. Once it does, this God's-eye view from above thrills them.

We land and there's snow everywhere.

"I have just one goal for this trip," Julian says, "and that is to throw a snowball at his ass," pointing at Matteo. This goal, trust me, was amply met during our three days in Montana. They get their hands on plastic sleds and, in one afternoon, live an entire childhood previously denied them.

Before our talk at the university, we are interviewed by the local paper, and pictures are taken. Julian and Matteo speak movingly after my speech and receive a standing ovation. The packed crowd has so much honor and reverence for what these two abandoned kids have had to carry all their young lives.

There is a Mass that follows and, to my great embarrassment, the chaplain at the university ends the liturgy by inviting the congregation to come forward and lay hands on me for healing of my leukemia. This, as they say, is not my cup of tea. Mortified, I stand there as, one by one, folks come up. Generally, they just lay hands and are silent. Some say things, a blessing or a prayer. Matteo comes up. My head is inclined and eyes closed. He has my head in a vise grip, and he's trembling and squeezing it with all his might. He leans right into my ear as he does this and can barely speak through his crying.

"All I know," he whispers, enunciating with special care, "is that . . . I love you . . . so . . . fucking . . . much."

Now I'm crying.

(The next day he says, "'*Spensa* for that blessing I gave you. I don't know how to do 'em." I assure him it was the best of the bunch.)

The following day we begin our return home to Los Angeles. That morning, on the front page of the Helena newspaper, above the fold, is a photograph, in color, of the three of us, four columns wide, standing in the cold, wearing our Homeboy beanies and jackets.

GANG MEMBERS VISIT HELENA WITH A MESSAGE OF HOPE.

The homies can't believe it, and they squirrel away many copies of the paper. People in the hotel, at a restaurant, in the airport, greet Matteo and Julian as celebrities. People are stopping them, shaking their hands, congratulating them. The TSA agents at the airport stop what they're doing to come around and salute them.

"We give you a lot of credit."

"Congratulations on your courage."

The flight attendants make a big deal about "the celebrities on board" as we settle into our seats at the very back of the tiny plane. Matteo and Julian are seated together, and I'm across the aisle. Midtrek, I look over and see Julian, in the window seat, knocked out, asleep with his head leaning on Matteo's shoulder. Matteo is crying.

"What's wrong, *mijo*?"

He has the Montana newspaper resting on his lap. "I just read this article again." He can't speak for a second and silently puts his hand over his heart. "I don't know . . . it really gets to me. Makes me feel like I am somebody." He cries all the more. I lean across and whisper, "Well, that's because you *are* somebody."

Matteo and Julian had never been inside before. Now a new place of fellowship has been forged, some roof in Montana has

79

been ripped right open, and those outside have been let in. There is a brand-new, palpable sense of solidarity among equals, a beloved community. This is always the fruit of true compassion.

Thomas Merton has his epiphany on the corner of Sixth and Walnut in Lexington, Kentucky. "I was suddenly overwhelmed with the realization that I loved all those people, that they were mine and I theirs."

What gets to Matteo, in the end, is the truth of how closely bound we are together, dissolving the myth that we are separate at all.

* * *

The first wedding I ever did was in Cochabamba, Bolivia. It was a humble Quechua couple, and the Mass was in the main Jesuit church in the center of town. Standing room only with Quechua Indians in their absolute finest clothes. Quechua *cholas* in brightly colored hoopy skirts and shawls, with tiny bowler hats perched, at a tilt, on top of their pinched-back hair. Men in suits with white collars, unspeakably wide and starched, craning their necks beyond what seems natural. Communion time arrives, and I go to the couple.

They refuse to receive communion. I beg them. They will not budge. I go to the congregation and invite them to receive communion. Not one person comes forward. I beg and plead, but no one steps up. I discover later, with the help of some Jesuit scholastics, that the Indians' sense of cultural disparagement and toxic shame was total. Since the time of the Conquista, when the Spaniards "converted" the Indians, they baptized them, but no roofs ever got ripped open. This was to be their place—outside of communion—forever.

Maybe we call this the opposite of God.

*   *   *

I had a three-state set of speaking gigs and brought two older homies, rivals, Memo and Miguel, to help me do it. We were in Atlanta, DC, and finally Spring Hill College in Mobile, Alabama. After our last talk in the morning at the college, we meet a man named John who tells us of his ministry in Pritchard, Alabama, and invites us to go visit his community. We take two hours to drive and walk around in what I think is about the poorest place I've ever seen in the United States. Hovels and burned-out shacks and lots of people living in what people ought not to live in.

Memo and Miguel are positively bug-eyed as they walk around, meet people, and see a kind of poverty quite different than the one they know.

We return to the house where we're staying and have half an hour to pack before leaving for the airport and our return home. We all dispatch to our own rooms, and I throw my suitcase together. I look up, and Memo is standing in my doorway, crying. He is a very big man, had been a shot caller for his barrio, and has done things in and out of prison for which he feels great shame— harm as harm. The depth of his core wound is quite something to behold. Torture, unrivalled betrayal, chilling abandonment— there is little terror of which Memo would be unfamiliar.

He's weeping as he stands in my doorway, and I ask him what's happening.

"That visit, to Pritchard—I don't know, it got to me. It got inside of me. I mean [and he's crying a great deal here] how do we let people live like this?"

He pauses, then, "G, I don't know what's happening to me, but it's big. It's like, for the first time in my life, I feel, I don't know, what's the word . . . I feel compassion for what other people suffer."

Outcast. Victim and victimizer. Sheep without a shepherd. Memo finds his core wound and joins it to the Pritchard core wound. Entrails, involving the bowels, the deepest place in Memo finds solidarity in the starkest wound of others. Compassion is God. The pain of others having a purchase on his life. Memo would return, with other homies, to Pritchard many times. A beloved community of equals has been fostered and forged there, and the roofs just keep getting ripped off. Soon enough, there won't be anyone left outside.

4

Water, Oil, Flame

I suppose that the number of homies I've baptized over the decades is in the thousands. Gang members find themselves locked up and get around to doing things their parents didn't arrange for them. Homies are always walking up to me at Homeboy Industries or on the streets or in a jail, saying, "Remember? You baptized me!"

The moment of a homie's baptism can be an awakening, like the clearing of a new path. You can tell it's the gang member's declaration that life will thereafter look different because of this pronouncement and its symbols. Consequently, the moment of baptism is charged with import and nerves.

One day at Juvenile Hall, I am introduced to a kid I am to baptize. I have never met him, but he knows who I am. He is saucer-eyed and panicky and bouncing slightly up and down. I shake his hand.

"I'm proud to be the one baptizing you," I say.

He tears up a bit and won't let go of my hand and my eyes. "Clockwise," he says.

I always tell those to be baptized that they have little to do and should leave all the heavy lifting to me.

I tell this one homie, before his baptism at a probation camp, "All you have to say is your name when I ask for it. Then I'll ask, 'What do you ask of God's church?' and you just say, 'Baptism.'"

When the moment arrives at the beginning of the rite, I can tell this kid is in trouble. He's hyperventilating, and his constant jig suggests he didn't visit the men's room before.

"What is your name?" I ask, and the kid booms back at me, "JOSE LOPEZ."

"And what do you ask of God's church, Jose?"

He stands erect, and his whole being wants to get this one right. "I WANT TO BE A BAPTIST."

I suggest he walk down the hall to the Protestant service.

Once, as I am about to baptize a kid at a probation camp, I ask him to incline his head over this huge pan of water, and he looks at me with shock and loudly asks, "You gonna WET me?"

"Uh, well, yeah . . . sorta the idea."

On a Saturday in 1996 I am set to baptize George at Camp Munz. He delays doing this with the other priests because he only wants me to do it. He also wants to schedule the event to follow his successful passing of the GED exam. He sees it as something of a twofer celebration. I actually know seventeen-year-old George and his nineteen-year-old brother, Cisco. Both are gang members from a barrio in the projects, but I have only really come to know George over his nine-month stint in this camp. I have watched him move gradually from his hardened posturing to being a man in possession of himself and his gifts. Taken out of the environment that keeps him unsettled and crazed, not surprisingly, he begins to thrive at Camp Munz. Now he is nearly unrecognizable. The hard *vato* with his gangster pose has morphed into a thoughtful, measured man, aware of gifts and talents previously obscured by the unreasonable demands of his gang life.

The Friday night before George's baptism, Cisco, George's brother, is walking home before midnight when the quiet is shattered, as it so often is in his neighborhood, by gunshots. Some rivals creep up and open fire, and Cisco falls in the middle of St. Louis Street, half a block from his apartment. He is killed instantly. His girlfriend, Annel, nearly eight months pregnant with their first child, runs outside. She cradles Cisco in her arms and lap, rocking him as if to sleep, and her screams syncopate with every motion forward. She continues this until the paramedics pry him away from her arms.

I don't sleep much that night. It occurs to me to cancel my presence at the Mass the next morning at Camp Munz to be with Cisco's grieving family. But then I remember George and his baptism.

When I arrive before Mass, with all the empty chairs in place in the mess hall, there is George standing by himself, holding his newly acquired GED certificate. He heads toward me, waving his GED and beaming. We hug each other. He is in a borrowed, ironed, crisp white shirt and a thin black tie. His pants are the regular, camp-issue camouflage, green and brown. I am *desvelado*, completely wiped out, yet trying to keep my excitement at pace with George's.

At the beginning of Mass, with the mess hall now packed, I ask him, "What is your name?"

"George Martinez," he says, with an overflow of confidence.

"And, George, what do you ask of God's church?"

"Baptism," he says with a steady, barely contained smile.

It is the most difficult baptism of my life. For as I pour water over George's head: "Father . . . Son . . . Spirit," I know I will walk George outside alone after and tell him what happened.

As I do, and I put my arm around him, I whisper gently as we walk out onto the baseball field, "George, your brother Cisco was killed last night."

I can feel all the air leave his body as he heaves a sigh that finds itself a sob in an instant. We land on a bench. His face seeks refuge in his open palms, and he sobs quietly. Most notable is what isn't present in his rocking and gentle wailing. I've been in this place before many times. There is always flailing and rage and promises to avenge things. There is none of this in George. It is as if the commitment he has just made in water, oil, and flame has taken hold and his grief is pure and true and more resembles the heartbreak of God. George seems to offer proof of the efficacy of this thing we call sacrament, and he manages to hold all the complexity of this great sadness, right here, on this bench, in his tender weeping. I had previously asked him in the baptismal rite, after outlining the contours of faith and the commitment "to live as though this truth was true." "Do you clearly understand what you are doing?"

And he pauses, and he revs himself up in a gathering of self and soul and says, "Yes, I do."

And, yes, he does. In the monastic tradition, the highest form of sanctity is to live in hell and not lose hope. George clings to his hope and his faith and his GED certificate and chooses to march, resilient, into his future.

What is the delivery system for resilience? In part, it's the loving, caring adult who pays attention. It's the community of unconditional love, representing the very "no matter whatness" of God. They say that an educated inmate will not reoffend. This is not because an education assures that this guy will get hired somewhere. It is because his view is larger and more educated, so that he can be rejected at ninety-three job interviews and still not give up. He's acquired resilience.

Sometimes resilience arrives in the moment you discover your own unshakeable goodness. Poet Galway Kinnell writes, "Sometimes it's necessary to reteach a thing its loveliness."

And when that happens, we begin to foster tenderness for our own human predicament. A spacious and undefended heart finds room for everything you are and carves space for everybody else.

* * *

I had a twenty-three-year-old homie named Miguel working for me on our graffiti crew. As with a great many of our workers, I had met him years earlier while he was detained. He was an extremely nice kid, whose pleasantness was made all the more remarkable by the fact that he had been completely abandoned by his family. Prior to their rejection of him, they had mistreated, abused, and scarred him plenty. He calls me one New Year's Day. "Happy New Year, G."

"Hey, that's very thoughtful of ya, dog," I say. "You know, Miguel, I was thinkin' of ya—you know, on Christmas. So, whad ya do for Christmas?" I asked knowing that he had no family to welcome him in.

"Oh, you know, I was just right here," meaning his tiny little apartment, where he lives alone.

"All by yourself?" I ask.

"Oh no," he quickly says, "I invited homies from the crew—you know, *vatos* like me who didn't had no place to go for Christmas."

He names the five homies who came over—all former enemies from rival gangs.

"Really," I tell him, "that sure was nice of you."

But he's got me revved and curious now. "So," I ask him, "what did you do?"

"Well," he says, "you're not gonna believe this . . . but . . . I cooked a turkey." You can feel his pride right through the phone.

"Wow, you did? Well, how did you prepare it?"

"You know," he says, "Ghetto-style."

I tell him that I'm not really familiar with this recipe.

He's more than happy to give up his secret. "Yeah, well, you just rub it with a gang a' butter, throw a bunch a' salt and pepper on it, squeeze a couple of *limones* over it and put it in the oven. It tasted proper."

I said, "Wow, that's impressive. What else did you have besides the turkey?"

"Just that. Just turkey," he says. His voice tapers to a hush. "Yeah. The six of us, we just sat there, staring at the oven, waiting for the turkey to be done."

One would be hard-pressed to imagine something more sacred and ordinary than these six orphans staring at an oven together. It is the entire law and the prophets, all in one moment, right there, in this humble, holy kitchen.

Not long after this, I give Miguel a ride home after work. I had long been curious about Miguel's own certain resilience. When we arrive at his apartment, I say, "Can I ask you a question? How do you do it? I mean, given all that you've been through—all the pain and stuff you've suffered—how are you like the way you are?"

I genuinely want to know and Miguel has his answer at the ready. "You know, I always suspected that there was something of goodness in me, but I just couldn't find it. Until one day,"—he quiets a bit—"one day, I discovered it here, in my heart. I found it . . . goodness. And ever since that day, I have always known who I was." He pauses, caught short by his own truth, (reteaching loveliness) and turns and looks at me. "And now, nothing can touch me."

The poet writes, "Someone fills the cup in front of us, we taste only sacredness." And the world will throw at us what it will, and we cling to our own sacredness, and nothing can touch us. But as I mentioned earlier, there is a lethal absence of hope in the gang member. There is a failure to conjure up the necessary image that can catapult you into your future. In fact, gang members form an exclusive club of young people who plan their funerals and not their futures.

In the late '80s we had a dance at the parish hall for young folks (soon the intensity of gang strife would make such dances a thing of the past).

A sixteen-year-old homegirl named Terry, a natural beauty and the object of every homie's longing, was dressed in this magnificent, short, bright red dress. She greets me at the door, where I provide security. She is radiant, and the toughness often on display in the streets has been left at home. I tell her how gorgeous she looks.

"Promise me something, G," she says, giddy and enlivened by all the compliments she's getting. "Promise me, that I get buried in this dress."

I'm instantly imagining the ridiculous snapshot of an old woman, at repose in her coffin, in a dress like this. But Terry envisions no such old woman.

An equally young homegirl bounds into my office one day to tell me she's pregnant. I suppose my face telegraphed, a little too clearly, a decided downsizing of my heart. Before I can say whatever I was going to say, she holds out her hand, as if to impede the words.

"I just want to have a kid before I die."

I'm thinking, *How does a sixteen-year-old get off thinking that she won't see eighteen?* It is one of the explanations for teen pregnancies in the barrio. If you don't believe you will reach eighteen, then you accelerate the whole process, and you become a mother well before you're ready.

In my earliest days, when gang violence had me burying more young people than old folks, I would often isolate the kid who had just viewed his dead homeboy in the casket. Maybe he's off by himself, crying and avoiding his *camaradas*. I figure perhaps I can speak a word to jostle him from his entrenched vow to seek revenge. Perhaps this is the vulnerable moment, a window cracked open to me. I would almost always say something like, "I never want to see you lying in a coffin at sixteen" or whatever his age is. When I first did this, I always expected the same response. "Yeah—that makes two of us. I don't want to die." What was initially startling grew predictable as I buried more kids. For this vulnerable one would always say the same thing, with little variation. "Why not—you gotta die sometime." This is the language of the despondent, for whom both hope and one's own sacredness are entirely foreign.

I remain always curious about the presence (or lack thereof) of the fathers in the lives of the homies. In the soul of nearly every homie I know there is a hole that's in the shape of his dad. Homeboy Industries is always trying to create the moment of what psychologists call the "sustenance of that first attachment." It is an offering (better late than never) of that parent-child bond that tells the fatherless that they're lovable.

The Japanese speak of a concept called *amae,* living in a deep sense of being cherished, of raising kids lovingly. I had asked one of my workers, David, about his father. David was not long released from camp, still on probation, and was cleaning the office after school as one of our part-timers.

"Oh," he says, monotone in place, accustomed as he was to answering this question, "he walked out on us." Then he shakes up the dial tone of his voice and wants to go deeper, truer than he has before.

"In fact the day he chose to walk out on us was my sixth birthday." There is a death behind his eyes that he can't mask. "We had a cake *y todo,* but I wouldn't let them cut it. I waited for my *jefito* to come home. I waited and waited. Nighttime came. He never did."

He pauses here for what I presume will be the moment for him to cry, but there is only dryness and a rage you can measure, the needle bouncing to its farthest edge.

"I cried till I was nine."

I wait for some emotional creaking here. Nothing.

"I don't cry anymore. I just hate him." The great encounter with the "father wound" is every homeboy's homework.

"When I was ten years old, I walked in on my dad, and he had a needle in his arm, all dazed. He looked at me and said, 'Take a good look. This will be you one day.'"

91

Another says, "My dad would fuck us up. I mean, fuck . . . us . . . up. You know, if we didn't massage his feet right or bring his wallet fast enough. I decided one day, 'I don't want to become him.'"

Still another, "I wish I never knew his name—wish I had never seen his face."

There is a wound that needs excavating before that "first attachment" can attach itself elsewhere.

* * *

Natalie came to work in our organization after keeping up a fairly regular correspondence with me over her years of incarceration. Through placement, juvenile hall, probation camp, and jail, she always let me know where she was, and I had never seen her "on the outs" until she finally walked through my door. Natalie was a runaway, a gang member, a regular drug user, and had two kids who had never been raised by her.

Once, while a group of us were approaching Pepperdine University, Natalie pointed down toward the beach and started to get excited. "Oooh—down there—I was in a summer camp there. Yeah, it was a camp for bad kids." Her parents were in and out but mainly out of her life since they all had arrived from Cuba.

"Yeah, we came on the Mariel Boatlift. You know, when Castro sent all the bad people here."

Her time working at our place has been pocked by moments of incarceration, suspensions for getting high, and even a handful of terminations for fighting. There was also a moment when I asked her not to come into the office—she would pick too many beefs with people. It was easier to get a call and then meet her at Jim's Burgers across the street. She was a handful to say the very least. She was one of the countless "what if" kids. What if she had actually been parented? What if she was surrounded by love and as much attention as a kid needs? What if she just had a stable place to rest her head?

I was on the road, somewhere in another time zone, giving a talk, and I had this vivid dream about Natalie. In some hotel lobby before giving a keynote address, I knew I had to locate her before it was my time to go on.

I catch her on her cell.

"Hey, kiddo, I had a dream about you last night."

"Oh no,"—dread filling her voice—"is it bad?" (All homies think dreams are omens and predictors of bad things to come.)

"No, no," I assure her, "It was a *firme* dream." I tell her that in the dream I am in this small club, not unlike a tiny comedy club, with small tables and a stage with a microphone. The emcee approaches the mike and quiets the crowd. "Ladies and gentlemen, to sing for you this evening, Ms. Natalie Urritia."

The boos are spontaneous and full. The crowd turns on me, for some reason. "What the hell's goin' on?" they ask me. "You know she can't sing worth shit—stop her."

I shrug and say nothing. I remember feeling nervous for her, but I don't intervene. The spotlight follows a gorgeous Natalie as she makes her way to the microphone. She is petite and fair skinned. She's in a dazzling, bejeweled dress, long and slinky. There seems to be no confidence in her at all, and the crowd all but throws things at her—howling and derisive. The music begins.

"And you start to sing, kiddo, and it's the most beautiful thing you ever heard in your life. It straight out shuts every damn body up. The crowd is silent, and our mouths are open. And none of us can believe this is you singing. But it's stunning—takes your breath away." I stop talking and she's silent.

"And . . . then I woke up."

There is such a hush you would have thought she had left me long ago.

"You're crying aren't you?"

"'Course," she squeaks.

And the soul quickens at hearing what it didn't know it already knew. Kathleen Norris writes, "If holding your ground is what you are called to most days, it helps to know your ground."

Resilience is born by grounding yourself in your own loveliness, hitting notes you thought were way out of your range.

*   *   *

Gangs are bastions of conditional love—one false move, and you find yourself outside. Slights are remembered, errors in judgment held against you forever. If a homie doesn't step up to the plate, perform the required duty, he can be relegated to "no good" status. This is a state from which it is hard to recover. Homeboy Industries seeks to be a community of unconditional love. Community will always trump gang any day.

Derek Walcott writes, "Either I am a nobody or I am a nation."

Our place at Homeboy is this touchstone of resilience. You discover your true self in this "nation." Homies who used to work at Homeboy always return on their days off or on their lunch break. A homie said to me once, "I just came by to get my fix."

"Of what?" I ask him.

"Love," he says.

Everyone is just looking to be told that who he or she is is right and true and wholly acceptable. No need to tinker and tweak. Exactly right.

* * *

I am working at my desk one day, eyes poring over something. You know how you can feel when two eyeballs are staring at you. I look up and it's Danny. He's a short, chubby ten-year-old who lives in the projects and is one of the fixtures around the office. A goofy, likable kid who does not do well in school. He seems to have purloined this oversize sketch pad, nearly as large as he is. He has it resting on his arched knee, and in his right hand is a pencil. He's sketching me. He works furiously on this drawing and then positions his pencil, held up at me, as if to size up the subject of his portrait. This is a technique he has retrieved, no doubt, from cartoons. He works on the portrait and then stops and holds his thumb and pencil at me to, again, capture my essence. This cracks me up. It is completely charming and funny. So I laugh.

Danny gets quite annoyed, "Don't move," he says, with not a little bit of menace.

Well, this makes me laugh all the more to think it makes any damn difference if I move. I'm howling a lot now. Danny turns steely on me, not the least bit amused. He becomes a clench-toothed Clint Eastwood. "I said, 'Don't move.'"

I freeze. I stop laughing, and he finishes his portrait.

Danny rips the sheet and lays the thing on my desk, revealing his *obra de arte*. And there in the middle of this huge piece of paper, about the size of a grapefruit, is me, I guess. Apparently,

I've been beat down with the proverbial ugly stick. It is Picasso on his worst day. My glasses are crooked, my eyes not at all where they should be. My face is generally woppy-jawed, and it is an unrecognizable mess. I'm kind of speechless. "Uh, wow, Danny, um . . . this is me?"

"Yep," he says, standing proudly in front of my desk, awaiting a fuller verdict.

"Wow, I hardly know what to say . . . I mean . . . it's . . . uh . . . very interesting." Danny looks a little miffed. "Well, whad ya spect. YA MOVED."

We squirm in the face of our sacredness, and a true community screams a collective "don't move." The admonition not to move is nothing less than God's own satisfaction at the sacredness, the loveliness that's there in each one—despite what seems to be a shape that's less than perfect.

* * *

Though he'd run away from home at thirteen, I only met Andres at nineteen after he had overstayed his welcome in various houses around town. Running away had seemed like the only reasonable thing to do. His mom, seeing in Andres the picture of his father, the man who had walked out on her, funneled all of her rage and disdain right at this kid. He became this male Cinderella, slavishly mopping the floors and bathroom of the bar she owned and the small apartment they shared. She didn't exactly abuse him. She tortured him. Putting cigarettes out on him, holding his head in the toilet until he nearly drowned. Andres was removed many times from the home by Child Protectors and just as routinely returned to her care.

Once he ran away, he aligned his misery with likely *camaradas* in a local gang—all hanging on for dear life and sharing the tight confines of their orphan island. When I met him, he was feeling the pressure to "move outta the homie's pad."

We had a shelter for women and children at the time, Casa Miguel Pro, nestled atop the elementary school, in what was the Dolores Mission convent. We had an extra room, and I gave it to Andres. Before long, he was employed, someone had donated a "tore up *ranfla*," so he had wheels for work, and he generally began to thrive.

Andres was one of those interviewed by Mike Wallace. Since I was to do tertianship—a yearlong break of reflection, prayer, long retreat, and ministry required of all Jesuits before they take final vows—and leave for a time after my tour as pastor, Mike asks Andres, now twenty-one, "You know, Father Greg says you're a success story. And he's leaving. I mean, are you going to continue on this path of success after Father Greg leaves?" Before Andres can address the question, Wallace inexplicably hunkers closer to Andres, seeking some inside-track camaraderie he frankly hasn't earned, and says, "You know, you'd really have to be an asshole not to continue on this path of success." Andres perks like a lion who hears someone coming. "What you call me?" Mike shifts in his metal folding chair like someone had just turned its heating element to high.

"Um, well, it's just a figure of speech; I mean, I'm not calling you that. It's just . . . well . . . ONE . . . would have to be an asshole . . ."

Andres is trembling at this point, his linebacker body wanting to go in eight directions at once. "There is only one person who can call me that . . . and that's Father Greg . . . not my family, not even my homies . . . but certainly not some rich white boy like you." Andres rips the microphone off his shirt and pounds his way to the side exit of the church where the interview was taking place. Mike's nervous aides pounce on my office. "Andres is mad." When I locate him, he won't let his ire be tamed. "I was gonna toss him up, G. I was gonna . . . straight out . . . toss him up." Let's face it, who among us hasn't wanted to "toss up" Mike Wallace?

Andres was alive, vibrant, and thriving as never before, and for the first time ever, there was a lightness to his being. He was proud of himself.

One day we bump into each other in the church parking lot.

"Ya know, I'm thinkin' a callin' my *jefita*."

"You sure?" I caution. After all, it had been more than five years since he had spoken with her.

"Well, yeah," he says, "I mean, she is the only mom I got."

I be-my-guest him toward my office, and I leave him. Not five minutes later, Andres is standing by my side again, looking stricken. This is what the woman who brought Andres into the world chose to say to her son, after not having spoken with or seen him for more than five years. This and only this.

"*Tú eres basura.*" (You are garbage.)

Now I'm stricken, barely able to hollow out a place in my own heart for such a thing as this. Andres's eyes glisten in the midday sun.

"You didn't believe her, did you?"

"Nah . . . I forgave her."

Years and years later, Andres plops in one of the chairs in my office, car in the shop (he'd been through many vehicles since that first bucket) and he's bussing it. He wanted to stop by and kick it before taking the bus home to his simple apartment. I offer to drive him home to Montebello.

"Would you mind, G, if we can swing by Ralph's so I can get some stuff? I mean, since I got a ride and all."

We pull into Ralph's, and I watch, always several steps behind, as Andres grabs a shopping cart and commandeers it down aisles of produce and canned goods. When I catch up with him, he says, "Tuesdays are the sales—that's the day to shop." I'm astonished at his assurance and utter familiarity with this place. He knows where to go. He knows what to get. He turns, I'm out of breath keeping up. He's in a confiding mood.

"Ya know, ya gotta be very careful in these big supermarkets."

"You do?" I say, leaning in to catch his drift.

"Oh, hell yeah."

Andres sizes up the aisle to see if there are spies. "It's that elevator music they be playing." He's whispering and pointing above. "It confuses you. Ya buy shit you don't need."

Home sweet home in his own skin. A man who has decided to walk in his own footsteps. God eternally satisfied with all his sacredness. Andres, a temple on high, a holy of holies, right there, on aisle 5.

Don't move.

*   *   *

I was praising a homie for one thing or another on the phone, and he just wouldn't have it. "You know," he insists, "I still have my blemishes." We still have to put our Western minds in a headlock and wrestle them to the ground. We think "blemishes" are shortcomings. We think our continually gnarly hardwired responses are not just proof of our humanity but (somehow) of our unworthiness. Homies are particularly culpable here. In an acute gangster version of the Stockholm syndrome, homies identify with, and grow attached to, their weaknesses and difficulties and burdens. You hope, in the light of this, to shift their attention and allegiance to their own basic goodness. You show them the bright blue sky of their sacredness, and they are transfixed only by the ominous clouds. You stand there with them and encourage them to stare above and wait twenty minutes.

"You are the sky," as Pema Chödrön would insist. "Everything else, it's just weather."

* * *

It would not be uncommon to ask Fabian how he's doing and then hear him respond, "I'm feeling zestfully clean, thank you." It may go without saying that I have never encountered a homie quite like Fabian. Few homeboys are able to incorporate in conversation, "Pip, pip, cheerio" or belittle your obvious response to something with, "Elementary, my dear Watson."

Fabian, now in his late twenties and married with three kids, worked for years at Homeboy Industries. Now he has a well-paying job and is as decent a human being as I know. He's just so uniquely a person like no other. He can, from memory, do the entire "shrimp montage" from *Forrest Gump*. He has also memorized every story from my talks.

Once I called him from Palm Springs, seconds before I was to "go on" and I was stumped. I couldn't remember the exact wording on something. He didn't even have to think about it, he handed the phrasing right to me.

His childhood was a dense mix of gangster father, mentally ill mother, and no one ever really in their *cinco sentidos*—always high, all the time. When he was ten or so, his mother was beating him with her high heel, when he sought refuge in the closet. She commenced to beat on Fabian's brother, Michael, and when his brother's screaming stopped, he peeked out of the closet and saw that his mother had wrapped a wire hanger around his neck, and he was turning blue. Fabian flew to her and body-slammed and wrestled her to the ground. Consequently, no one would have been surprised if Fabian had taken up permanent residence in some state-run, locked-down facility.

But somehow, by a mysterious and gracious turn of some steering wheel, Fabian found other coordinates and navigated his way out of the treacherous waters where others perished.

His brand of humor is so smart and odd that one occasionally suspects that some alien has taken possession of this homeboy. Traveling in DC to speak in front of a congressional subcommittee, Fabian and Felipe, an enemy from his gang's worst rival, were kicking it upstairs at my brother Paul's house, watching *Gremlins*.

Paul and his wife, Joy, and I were sipping beers after a long day. Fabian, nineteen at the time, came down the stairs to get sodas for himself and Felipe. He goes directly to the refrigerator, making himself at home, but stops when he sees us.

"Can I have a beer?"

"No."

Fabian reaches in to get his Cokes. Then stops.

"It would mean a lot to me."

"Nope."

He digs deeper into the fridge and then pulls himself out of there.

"I would cherish this moment?"

I ask you, who talks like this?

Just recently, we were on the phone. He is forever calling and checking in and the conversations rapidly dissolve into a swirling sink of silliness.

I am ready to deal with all the people lined up to see me in my office, so I try to extricate myself from Fabian's clutches.

"Well," I say to him, "it will be my great pleasure to hang up on your ass right now."

He feigns "Why I never . . ." huffiness.

Then, "Well, it will be MY great pleasure to be HUNGEN up by you."

"Good comeback," I tell him.

Fabian was spectacular at building good and enduring friendships with his "enemies" at Homeboy. His tenderness knew no equal, really. He would visit an enemy undergoing brutal chemotherapy and supply him with videos to distract him from the ordeal. He'd do reconnaissance of the hospital area to make sure that none of his enemies were also visiting at the same time.

His enemies wouldn't understand. Once, Fabian was stuck in the backseat of a car filled with his homeboys who were giving him a ride home.

"Hey, look," one of them screams in the car, "that's that fool,

Froggy." The alarmist in the car is pointing at an enemy walking by himself on First Street. "Let's bomb on his ass."

The car pulls over, and Fabian works his magic. "Kick back, you guys. That's my *primo*."

"*Serio*, he's your cousin?"

"Yeah—my *tia*'s son."

And the car swerves back into merging traffic. Froggy was an enemy Fabian had come to know from our office. They are not related.

I just don't know how Fabian managed it.

With more mystery than I can explain away, Fabian locked on to the singularity of that love that melts you. It doesn't melt who you are, but who you are not. Turns out he wasn't all the abuse he endured. He was something else, astonishing and glorious.

* * *

For two decades I've been working with gang members, and, on occasion, it occurs to people to present me with some award or another. I've gotten a number of these over the years—a bronze lion, a crystal "catchyvatchy," a plaque, or framed acknowledgement. (Especially in recent years, with a cancer diagnosis, you start getting "lifetime achievement awards"—if you know what I mean.) I've never kept one of these.

I always give them to one of the homies. Usually there is a fancy dinner at some Beverly Hills hotel. They give me a table, and I fill it with half homies and half ladies from the projects. They are dressed in their absolute finery. The women in dresses they wore at their daughters' *quinceañeras*, the homies in perfectly ironed Ben Davis pants and large, untucked plaid shirts. Gangster standard issue. They become intrigued by the amount of silverware at their place settings. "What's this fork for?" They invariably ask the waiter for Tapatío hot sauce. When the gourmet arugula and pear balsamic vinegar salad arrives, they dive in, and someone weighs in, "This shit tastes nasty."

Someone always says this.

After the event, I drive everyone home, knowing that the last homie I drop off is the one to whom I'll give the award. (Once, I gave a magnificent ornate plaque to a homie, and he said, "Wow—this is great. And when you kick rocks, I'll sell it on eBay and make a grip a' *feria* [money]."

When I get to the last house with the last homie, I say, "Hey, dog, you're my hero—look where you've been and where you are now. So, I want you to have . . . this bronze lion."

I tell him that I'll come visit it from time to time.

I had been invited to receive some award from the Education Department at Loyola Marymount University. I had a speaking engagement up north at the same time, so I asked if I could send one of my workers to receive it on my behalf (knowing that I would have him keep the award afterward).

The LMU people agreed, and I selected Elias to accept my *premio.* Elias was eighteen years old, working at Homeboy Silkscreen, and had traded in his gang past for fatherhood and gainful employment. Given the horror show that was his family, environment, and the number of obstacles on his road along the way, his success was all the more astonishing.

"Could you go to this event and accept this award on my behalf," I ask him.

He's taken aback by the honor, "'Course I will."

"Oh, by the way," I continue, "Ya gotta give a little acceptance speech." His eyes widen. "WHAT?"

I tell him to relax, to write a couple of paragraphs, and he'll be fine. I tell him that Cara Gould, one of our senior staff at the time (and among the most skilled at working with homies I've ever seen), will take him to LMU.

I hear later that the trip to the awards evening is Panic Central. Elias wants to leap from the moving car. This is how nervous he is. "Cara, I can't do it. I can't speak in front of these people."

Cara tries to calm him some. "Look," she says, "they always say that if you're nervous speaking in front of people, just imagine your entire audience is stark naked."

Elias turns on her. "I CAN'T DO THAT—I'd be staring the whole time."

Once they get to the auditorium, things move from bad to worse. The place is packed. Standing room only. Flop sweat dots Elias's forehead. The emcee says, "Accepting the award on behalf of Father Greg Boyle is Elias Montes."

The crowd claps warmly as Elias awkwardly makes his way to the podium, bathed in a spotlight. He's trembling as he holds the yellow lined paper on which he's written his speech. It's not much of a speech, really. There is no poetry, only the unmistakable testimony of this kid standing there—transformed and astonishing. The audience seems to get this on the first bounce. He gets to the end with a big finish. "Because Father Greg and Homeboy Industries believed in me, I decided to believe in myself. And the best way I can think of payin' 'em back is by changing my life. And that's exactly what I've decided to do. Thank you."

The auditorium erupts in applause. They truly go nuts. They are on their feet and people are crying and shouting. Folks are locating their Kleenex and will not stop clapping. Elias finds his seat. Cara is standing next to him, crying a great deal, but so is the man on the other side of Elias. The ovation continues, and Elias is quite oblivious to it all. Finally, he leans into Cara, who is still standing and applauding with the others, and whispers, "Damn, they're sure clappin' a lot for G."

Cara crouches toward him, *"Oye, menso,* they're not clappin' for G—they're clappin' for YOU."

Elias straightens as if connected to a power plant.

"NUH-UH," he says.

"Yeah, huh," Cara says. "They are clapping for you."

And so, an entire room of total strangers hands Elias back to himself and says in no uncertain terms, "Don't move."

* * *

Jason's appearance in my office was a first. Though I had known him most of his life, he was an expert at resisting my offers of help. In the interim, Jason had done his share of dirt for his gang. He would rather be employed selling crack than in anything else. He was cemented in his resistance to me. And yet there he was, that day, in my office.

"Y ese milagro?"—"I can't believe you're here," I say.

Jason was uncharacteristically quiet, humble in the face of whatever it was that was happening to him. I wish I could flesh out more why and how Jason managed to show up in my office that day. It's all quite mysterious to me. With my ear to the ground, I knew only his total commitment to his barrio and drug-dealing and general criminality. I couldn't draw a straight line between the fact of his appearance in my office that day and some pivotal, recent moment in the past. I still could only see the goofy kid I had met fifteen years earlier, who had no recourse but to let the streets raise him.

I send him to one of our job developers who in turn sends him to a job interview that very day. Not two hours later, he's back, brimming with excitement.

He stands in the doorway of my office, "I GOT THE JOB!"

"That's great," I say.

"Yeah," he says, "The manager said I fit the description."

He's got me here. "Well, I suppose," I say, "if you're America's Most Wanted, he might have said, 'fit the description.' Or did he say, you 'met the qualifications'?"

Jason convulses, giggles, and slaps his forehead. "Yeah, dat one—'met the qualifications'—sheesh—what was I thinkin' 'fit the description'—stooopid."

Jason dropped by often after that. To just get "his fix," I suppose. Hoping to get an even better job, he'd get help with his résumé. More often than not, he'd just check in with me. This seemed easy for him, no longer saddled with the shame of his previous "knucklehead" existence, he held his head high and could face me. He could gaze at himself in the mirror and not move. It had been a long time (if ever) since he was able to do that.

"I finally realized why I was out there so long," he tells me in one of his visits, referring to his gangbanging and drug-dealing.

"Yeah, I can see why now. It's just, I was so fuckin' angry all the time."

And of course why wouldn't he be? Both parents were heroin addicts, and he was left to raise himself—which kids are meant not to be good at.

"And now," he says, "I just let it all go—the anger, I mean."

In one of his drop-bys on a Wednesday, I ask him, "So, are we all set for your daughter's baptism on Saturday?"

"Oh yeah," he says, "I bought the dress yesterday. She's gonna look beautiful."

The next morning, on the way to a job interview for a better position, Jason was gunned down. Someone drove by and saw him and perhaps all his past had become present again. I buried him a week later and baptized his daughter at his funeral Mass. Water, oil, flame.

I landed on the gospel that I wanted to use at his liturgy. Jesus says, "You are the light of the world." I like even more what Jesus doesn't say. He does not say, *"One day, if you are more perfect and try really hard, you'll be light."* He doesn't say *"If you play by the rules, cross your T's and dot your I's, then maybe you'll become light."* No. He says, straight out, "You are light." It is the truth of who you are, waiting only for you to discover it. So, for God's sake, don't move. No need to contort yourself to be anything other than who you are. Jason was who he was. He made a lot of mistakes, he was not perfect, and his rage called the shots for a goodly chunk of his life. And he was the light of the world. He fit the description.

5

Slow Work

David had decided to change. Sixteen years old, back in school for the first time "in the longest" and working part-time for me at Homeboy, David liked living in his own skin again—or perhaps for the first time. He enjoyed being as smart as he was discovering himself to be.

One day he lands in my office and seems to want to try his hand at small talk.

"You know," he says, "I ran into a man who attended one of your talks recently."

I give a lot of talks, and David has accompanied me several times.

"Really," I say, "that's nice."

"Yep," he says, "he found your talk . . . rather monotonous."

"Gosh," I say, with some dismay, "really? He did?"

"Weeellll, actually," David says, "that didn't happen. But I just need practice using bigger words."

I suggest that he practice on somebody else.

*   *   *

In 12-step recovery programs they often say, "It takes what it takes." This is true enough when it comes to change. The light-bulb appears and it brightens. Who can explain how or when? We can't do this for each other. David just decided.

After Mass at Central Juvenile Hall in Los Angeles, I spot a kid named Omar, seventeen years old, whom I had known for some years. I actually never knew him "on the outs"—only in a variety of detention facilities like the halls or camps or in a placement. He never seemed to be out very long before he'd find himself swept up, yet again, in gangbanging and life on the streets.

He gesticulates wildly at me, as he is being led back to his unit. "Come see me." He mouths his unit, "KL."

I locate Omar in the dayroom of Unit KL. He knows the drill. He quickly sweeps up two plastic chairs, whose backs are carved with gang graffiti, and carries them away from the others, land-ing near the windows, out of earshot. He tells me he'll be leaving on Thursday, and I can't help but think I will be bumping into him yet again in one of these county-controlled facilities. After a half hour, I eye the clock on the wall and tell Omar, "Gotta go, dog."

"Why so fast, G?" he asks. I stand.

"I have an anniversary Mass at the cemetery for a homie I bur-ied a year ago. So, gotta go."

Omar stays seated and is uncharacteristically pensive.

"Hey, G," he says. "Can I ask ya a question?"

"Sure, *mijo*," I say, "Anything."

"How many homies have you buried . . . you know, killed because of gangbanging?

"Seventy-five, son." (This was some years ago. If he asked today, it would be more than twice that number.)

"Damn, G, seventy-five?" He shakes his head in disbelief, his voice a bare hush now. "I mean, damn . . . when's it gonna end?"

I reach down to Omar and go to shake his hand. We connect and I pull him to his feet. I hold his hand with both of mine and zero in on his eyes.

"*Mijo*, it will end," I say, "the minute . . . you decide."

The moistening of his eyes surprises me. He grabs my hands in his.

"Well," he says, "then, I decide."

"Omar," I tell him, "it has always been as simple as that."

"How many things have to happen to you," Robert Frost writes, "before something occurs to you?"

Change awaits us. What is decisive is our deciding.

* * *

Mass is about to begin at Camp Munz, and I've been shaking hands with the gathering homies filing into the gym. They are all dressed in their military fatigues, smiling and courteous. There is one kid covered in tattoos, face and arms, which is not usual with this young age group. I pull him out of line, and he says his name is Grumpy. He only offers his gang moniker and seems tougher on the first bounce than most kids are.

"Look," I say, fishing one of my cards from my pocket, "call me when you get out, and we'll remove your tattoos for free."

Now, usually when I say this, the response is nearly always the same. They grab the card and stare at it and say something like, "Really? . . . wow . . . for free? . . . *firme*." But not Grumpy. He doesn't take my card. He looks at me, as the homies would say, "all crazy," and on total LOUD status, says, "Yeah, well, why'd I get 'em if I'm just gonna take 'em off?" He's huffy and belligerent. This almost never happens. In the face of this rare occurrence, I become quite placid and find my preternatural calm voice.

"Well," I say, "I don't even know you—but I KNOW why you got all these tattoos."

"Yeah," louder still, he says, "Then why'd I get 'em?"

"Well, simple," I say, as quiet as he is loud, "One day, when you weren't looking, your head . . . got stuck . . . up your butt. That's right, dog, you straight-out keistered your *cabeza*. So," and I force my card into his hand, "you call me . . . the minute . . . you locate your head."

Not my proudest moment, but as the homies might say, "I don't let myself," which is to say, you get crazy with me, I tend to get crazy back. I'm working on it.

Some five months later, someone gives me a slew of Lakers tickets, enough to fill the parish van with the *pandilla mugrosa* (a group of trouble-making little ones from Pico Gardens, who all seemed to have a common allegiance to bad hygiene, an allergy to bathing). It was when the Lakers still played in the Forum, and we had been blessed with seats not in the nosebleed section, but in the cerebral hemorrhage section. The gaggle of project kids was running up ahead of me, but I took my time climbing the stairs. Suddenly, in about fifteen of the aisle seats, a group of Camp Munz youth all stand to salute me. "Hey, G," one says, "It's us from Camp Munz." They come into focus for me. They are all in their camouflage garb—given free tickets as well. I shake the hands of each one, seated all behind one another on the aisle. The hollering, "DOWN IN FRONT," does not make us speed up our greeting. We're all mutually excited to have bumped into one another. I'm nearing the end, and the third to the last *vato* is Grumpy. We fix on each other, and I extend my hand to his. He refuses to shake it. I think, *Not good.* There is a beat before, quite unexpectedly, Grumpy throws his arms around me and squeezes tight. He leans into my ear and whispers, "I get out Tuesday . . . I'll call ya Wednesday . . . I wantcha ta . . . take my tattoos off."

Teilhard de Chardin wrote that we must "trust in the slow work of God."

Ours is a God who waits. Who are we not to? It takes what it takes for the great turnaround. Wait for it.

*   *   *

In the early days, I was not always so good at waiting. I would find myself on my bike in the housing projects, coaxing and nudging homies to embrace the employment opportunities that would sometimes come my way. Leo was a case in point. More times than I can remember, I'd set something up.

"Okay, dog, I got an interview for you," I'd tell Leo, a nineteen-year-old dropout, who'd pass most of his day just kickin' it with his homies in the projects. Leo was a short, squat, exceedingly likable kid you could not resist wanting to help. Often I would set something up—an interview—a chance of a chance of something, and his enthusiasm never waned. "Yeah, *firme,*" he'd say. And when the designated moment arrived, Leo would leave me hangin' in the designated spot. I'd wait and he'd never show up. This happened to me more than a handful of times.

One evening, late, I'm standing with some homies in the darkness of one of the project archways. At some distance, in the nearby parking lot, I can see Leo running up to a car and making a sale. He's counting his money and walks toward our poorly lit archway. When he arrives, he looks up and is mortified to see me, to know that I've witnessed this entire transaction. The expression he's sporting is *cara de cachado*.

"'*Spensa*, G," he says, "*La neta*, I didn't even see you there. My bad."

"No need to apologize, *mijo*," I say to him. "You taught me something tonight."

"I did?" Leo says, confused, yet obviously interested.

"That's right," I say. "Tonight, you taught me that no amount of my wanting you to have a life is the same as you wanting to have one. Now, I can help you get a life—I just can't give you the desire to want one. So, when you want a life, call me."

And I walk away more than a little discouraged. I contemplate a career change—crossing guard perhaps.

Some months later, Leo did call me.

"It's time already," he says. I knew exactly what that meant.

"So, what caused the lightbulb to turn on?" I ask.

"Well . . . today . . . I was watching *Jerry Springer*."

Apparently, people throwing chairs at each other wakes your ass up—who knew?

"And they had a commercial 'bout that ITT Institute—where ya learn shit, and I think, maybe I'll call G, you know, and get me one a' them . . . careers."

Now Leo had a superhuman affinity for animals. He was the St. Francis of the projects. Though pets were not allowed in the projects, people had them nonetheless. Folks would bring their pets, the crippled dog or cat, and somehow Leo had his healing way with them. They'd "drop their crutches" and be good as new.

I'd just met a veterinarian at a talk I gave, so I called him. He hired Leo right away—first to clean up the dog poop and the cages. Then Leo learned to bathe the animals and even give them shots. Now he's a supervisor at an animal shelter. It wasn't long before Leo had got himself "one a' them . . . careers." It was worth the wait.

Sometimes you need to walk in the gang member's door, in order to introduce him to a brand-new door. You grab what he finds valuable and bend it around something else, a new form of nobility. You try to locate his moral code and conform it to a new standard that no longer includes violence and the harboring of enemies.

*   *   *

Anniversaries of the dead from barrios are honored and commemorated with great care. This was certainly true in my early days—when gangs were just beginning to see fatalities. These days, anniversaries seem to be less recalled than they were twenty years ago. As the number of homicides accelerates, only the families and close friends still seem to remember.

A homie named Psycho, nineteen, has been dead a month, and fifteen of his homies are insistent on going to Resurrection Cemetery to mark this thirty-day moment. I pile them all in the parish van, and we find the nearly fresh dirt and turf where we had gathered a month before. The family has yet to secure enough funds to place a *piedra* with his name, but the homies know where he is "resting in peace." In fact this becomes, for homies, the veritable last name of all their dead: "Psycho Rest-in-Peace."

"We went to visit the other day, Trigger Rest-in-Peace Mom," a homie might say. And it is very common for young women to identify themselves on the phone this way: "This is Blanca. Sniper Rest-in-Peace baby's mom."

We encircle the grave and no one speaks. The homies stand with their hands in their pockets and stare at the ground, this resting place. I look the other way as homies sneak off and steal flowers from other graves and place them on the ground in front of us. They smoke and several of them light a *frajo* for Psycho and then rest it burning on a tuft of grass below.

Carlos, a skinny and impossibly tall homie, not yet eighteen, starts to sob. The circle of us surrounding Psycho's marker is complete, and Carlos is now convulsing with a renewed grief, inconsolable in what has now become full-body heaving and wailing. I can sense the circle is disquieted by this. Footfalls shift and tap, and though no one looks at Carlos, they are all clearly uncomfortable with this display. I don't sense that they judge it false or inappropriate, only a manifestation of some gate they would rather not have opened. Sensing the signal the group is sending, I put my arm around Carlos and walk him away from the circle. He is awash in *mocos* and tears and seems not at all concerned with mopping up after himself. He sobs resolutely while I stand there with him, arm draped lightly over his shoulder. There is more than grief here. He tells me, between his insucks of breath and jags of crying, that he was with Psycho earlier in the day, before he was killed that night. Just the two of them walking in the hood.

It occurred to Psycho to tell Carlos of a premonition. He knows he is going to die soon. "But if anything happens to me," he tells Carlos, "I know you will take care of everything." Carlos has been carrying this for thirty days and has told no one. "Taking care of everything" only means one thing in gang parlance: kill the one who kills me. It means revenge—fast and sure and clear. Carlos is a pimply teenager who drank in excess and joined a gang some years earlier when he discovered that the man he thought was his father was, in fact, his stepdad. The earthquake of this revelation sent Carlos into an odd free fall, hardened anything that was soft, and somehow lodged him tight in this crevice of hard drinking and serious hanging with gangsters. At the core, though, he frankly didn't want to carry the burden of avenging this death.

"And you *have* taken care of everything," I whisper to him, trying desperately to find another door for him to exit. "I mean, who organized all the car washes that paid for his funeral? You did. Who has been so present to Psycho's mom and sister during this whole time? It was you. You hardly ever left their side, comforting them. Who has helped me more in calming down the homies so they don't do something stupid and regrettable? Only you, dog. Only you."

I lean on him and plead my case, my closing argument. "In fact, son, I think you may be the downest *vato* I've ever known. *Neta*. I mean, you took care of everything."

* * *

Homies get stuck so often in a morass of *desesperación,* both the impasse writ large and the ordinary mud of inertia. Few can conjure an image of something better. Joey is one of these stuckees. At twenty-one years old, he seems eternally adolescent, and he has mastered the art of hanging out. He is a cherubic-cheeked, chunky kid who looks forever twelve. He is halfhearted even in his sporadic forays into selling crack. He sells enough to feed himself at McDonald's and resume the ardors of just kicking it. The assertion in *Freakonomics* is true enough—that, by and large, very few homies are getting rich selling drugs. No one's buying the home in La Puente. Certainly not Joey. I try frequently to shake Joey out of this stupor of sleeping late, slinging a little, kicking it with the homies, checking in with his *jaina,* and enduring the "woofing" of his grandma. His more purposeful older brother, Memo, sums up Joey's level of maturity: "He always be actin' his shoe size—eight." This shiftlessness has become his life, and for all the pointing I make in the general direction of possible exits, all are politely shrugged away.

Joey shows up one morning at my office, and his smile seems to come from a deeper, surer place than usual.

"Get ready to be proud of me," he says, settling in.

"Okay, I'm sitting down—fire away."

"You are talking . . . to an employed *vato* right now."

"*Serio,* dog? *Felicidades.* So where you workin'?"

Joey turns around to make sure no one is lurking nearby.

"Now that's the thing, dog," he says, lowering his voice and moving closer to me. "You have to promise not to tell the homies."

I agree.

"Well, I'm workin' at Chuck E. Cheese," he tells me.

"Well . . . that's great, son," I assure him, feeling my nose grow. "But what do you do there?"

"But that's the thing, Gee, you can't tell the homies."

I nod.

"I'm the rat."

The mascot, a rat, IS Chuck E. Cheese.

"Wow . . . I mean that's great." I try and convince him . . . and myself.

"No, it ain't . . . it sucks. The rat suit is aaaallll hot, and it be hummin' in there, and the kids be buuuuuugggggiiinnnn. They be pushing you and putting *chicle* on you."

"*Pero, mijito*, I'm proud of you," I tell him, "But what woke you up enough to go apply for a job?"

Joey gets sober and clear-eyed, and there is no doubting, for him, how he was led to this moment and place and rat suit.

"In two months, my son's gonna be born. I want him to come into the world and meet his father—a workin' man."

That'll do it.

*   *   *

I always thought Bugsy was the perfect moniker for Jaime. He bugged. You could set your watch by the predictable, postjail visit. Bugsy was bound to ask for something minutes after rolling out of the county jail on Bauchet Street. He was tiny but scrappy, and though in his early twenties, having seen his slice of terror and trauma, he had old man's eyes. Since we have been in exactly this scene countless times before, Bugsy moves right to it.

"Here's the deal—check out my shoes, G. I mean they to'e up from the flo' up—do me that *paro*, yeah? And buy me some shoes?"

I figure the sheer repetition of this moment with Bugsy should come at some price to him.

"Ok, I'll buy you the shoes—but first you have to answer this question correctly."

Bugsy seems game.

"First, I have to set the stage, before I ask the question."

I am charmed by Bugsy's intensity; his attention is total.

"One day, the phone rings, and one of our workers, a sixteen-year-old homie named Manuel, answers it. 'Homeboy Industries, how may I help you?' Well, it's a collect call, and we always accept collect calls, so Manuel does. On the other end, calling from County Jail, is a twenty-year-old from an enemy neighborhood to Manuel—though neither knows this yet.

"'May I help you?' Manuel says to the twenty-year-old.

"The jailbird growls at him, 'WHO'S THIS?'

"Now Manuel thinks: '*I could say, "Lucky," my gang placa,*' but nah—so he says, 'Manuel.' And the twenty-year-old gets even more lokie.

"'WHERE YOU FROM?' (a provocative question, wanting to identify his gang).

"Manuel says, 'Please hold,' turns to Norma, my assistant, and says, 'Norma, could you handle line three, please?'"

Bugsy could not lean in more. To do so would put him on my side of the desk.

"Now," I continue, "That's the setup, and here's the question. Which of these two *vatos* was the REAL man? The sixteen-year-old or the guy who was twenty?"

Bugsy leans back now, and he knows he's getting a new pair of shoes.

"Oh, come on, G," he half-laughs, "That's easy."

"Well, then," I say, "Who?"

"Well, obviously, the sixteen-year-old."

"Why him and not the older *vato*?"

"Well, cuz the sixteen-year-old didn't play that little-kid

stuff—that gangbanging masa," he says, as dismissive as he could be of such behavior.

"Very good, my dog," I say to him. "I've got good news and bad news for you. The good news: you're getting brand-new shoes. The bad news: you know the twenty-year-old *vato*, calling from jail . . . THAT WAS YOU, *CABRÓN*, WHEN YOU CALLED COLLECT TWO MONTHS AGO!"

Bugsy winces slightly.

"Yeah, I sorta thought that's where this story was goin'."

*   *   *

There is nothing "once and for all" in any decision to change. Each day brings a new embarking. It's always a recalibration and a reassessing of attitude and the old, tired ways of proceeding, which are hard to shake for any of us.

These are the calls I cannot bear getting: "They're shooting in Aliso."

This one comes at midday, and I am sitting in my office, our reception room filled with homies in line to see me.

I excuse myself and race to my car. The details are these: Two gang members have entered enemy turf and are "crossing out" their enemy's *placas* (their gang monikers) when a group of *enemigos* spot them, holler, and begin to run toward them. One of the two invading homies pulls out a gun and shoots wildly, attempting to dissuade the approaching enemies on foot. No one is hurt, but a bullet does travel to our Alternative School (DMA) on Mission Road, punctures a window, and a shard of shattered glass slightly cuts the face of a mother who is in the school's office. She is taken to the hospital.

I'm not sure why I even go to the projects when I receive one of these calls. I suppose you go because you're called. I'm never entirely sure what people's expectation of me might be. You mainly just stand with folks as they catch their breath and wait for their blood pressure to settle. This day, traveling west down First Street with considerable speed, I see Johnny and Bear on the wrong side of the street, in enemy territory. They are shirt-less, running and desperate to get to the right side of the street. I know immediately these must be our marauding, spray-painting gang members. I get confirmation of this when they spot me driving toward them, and I can read their lips, "OH SHIT."

They stop and bolt down an alley. This incenses me. Sud-denly I am both Starsky *and* Hutch. I'm driving like I've placed a flashing red light on the top of my car, careening down the alley, narrowly nicking garbage cans and swerving to miss refuse and car parts. I see the shirtless ones take a left, and I follow. I don't know why I'm doing this. Quite apart from the infuriating mid-day shooting is the fact that they run when they see me. This is new and just pisses me off. I barrel out of the alley, and they're gone. I circle the neighborhood for some time and give up. I go to the scene of the shooting and calm down the aggrieved homies who have had their neighborhood dissed and check in with the school and make sure they are rebounding. I get a report of the woman with the piece of flying glass lodged in her cheek, and I go back to where I think I might find Johnny and Bear. I park and walk and turn a fortuitous corner, and there they are, sitting on the front porch of Bear's girlfriend's house. They get to their feet at the sight of me, and I hold out my hand to stop their flight and say quickly, "Nope" as in, "Oh, hell no—you are not going anywhere."

I summon them off the porch and signal them to join me by the short gate and fence that fronts the property. They are still shirtless, still sweating from their great escape.

"Don't you ever . . . run from me . . . again." I begin calmly and stay in this tone—though I'm as enraged as any father snatching his four-year-old out of the street as a car approaches. You don't realize how grateful you are that your kid is safe—you are just furious at what his wandering out there could have brought you all. I came to always feel this outsize stress—coming from some deep, primordial place within me—wanting to protect and yet feeling a Garpian dread that the "undertoad is strong today." *Pre*traumatic stress syndrome, if you will.

Even now, I spend much of the day just bracing myself. It's infuriating and death-defyingly stressful when, consciously or no, the kids you love cooperate in their own demise.

Johnny and Bear predictably have more remorse about fleeing me than they do about their foray into enemy turf. I have pieced things together enough to know that Johnny was the lone shooter. I turn to him and know exactly how I want this conversation to end. "Oh, by the way, Johnny, I thought maybe you'd want to know—no one was seriously hurt when you shot just now."

He neither protests nor proclaims his innocence. He just continues to listen with some intensity. "A woman was standing in the school office when one of your bullets shattered a window. A piece of glass cut her face, and she went to the hospital. She'll be okay. Just thought you'd like to know."

I walk away and say nothing more in my leave-taking. Then before I get very far, I come back. "Gosh, Johnny, I almost forgot this part. The woman with the cut face—yeah—that was your mom, son. *Your mom.* She'll be okay. Just . . . thought you'd like to know."

Johnny blanches at this, and all his blood drains right out of him, leaving him white and speechless. It only feels like Johnny and Bear think this is all a game—placing themselves in danger, recklessly firing a gun, holding in no regard the lives of so many. The outsider will invariably draw this conclusion. Yet they are comrades in despair, and their inability to care for their own lives consistently plays itself out in the abandonment of all reason and surely all hope.

* * *

There is no force in the world better able to alter anything from its course than love. Ruskin's comment that you can get someone to remove his coat more surely with a warm, gentle sun than with a cold, blistering wind is particularly apt. Meeting the world with a loving heart will determine what we find there. We mistakenly place our trust, too often, in the righteousness of our wind, though we rarely get evidence that this ever transforms anything. Inmate and guard alike at Folsom Prison (where I did a stint as chaplain) always said the same thing about the other: "I don't want them to mistake my kindness for weakness."

Sooner or later, we all discover that kindness is the only strength there is. I can remember listening to a kid at a probation camp read at Mass from 1 Corinthians 13. If you've been to as many weddings as I have, you go numb as you hear, "Love is patient. Love is kind. Love is blah, blah, blah." Your mind floats away. You start wondering if the Dodgers won last night and remind yourself to move your clothes from the washer to the dryer. But this kid started to read it like it mattered and it, as the homies would say, "woke my ass up proper." He looked out at everyone and proclaimed with astounding surety: "Love . . . never . . . fails."

And he sat down.

And I believed him.

Every day, you choose to believe this all over again and want only "to live as though the truth were true."

In my early, crazy days doing this work with gangs, I will admit I was totally out of whack. I'd ride my bike, in the middle of the night, in the projects, trying to put out fires ("Put that Uzi down"; "Now you sure you wanna shoot that guy?"). Trying to "save lives" is much like the guy spinning plates on *Ed Sullivan,* attempting to keep them from crashing to the floor. I'd look for the wobblers. Who was about to smash into a million pieces?— and then I'd be frantic to keep that homie from self-destructing. It was crazy-making, and I came close to the sun, to the immolation that comes from burning out completely in the delusion of actually "saving" people.

I took a break in 1992, and in the stillness of meditation and the sweetness of surrender I found a place of balance and perspective. I found consolation in a no doubt apocryphal story of Pope John XXIII. Apparently, at night he'd pray: "I've done everything I can today for your church. But it's Your church, and I'm going to bed."

Before, I guess I never really went to bed—available 24/7 to respond to any call and at the ready to talk homies off the ledge.

A touchstone story happened not long after I returned from my time off. A homie, Pedro, who works for me now as a case manager, was then a greatly troubled kid filled with a measured rage and resentment he submerged beneath first heavy drinking and then crack cocaine. Pedro, among the gentlest and most kindhearted of homies, disappeared, eventually, into his own netherworld of substance abuse. He was seemingly oblivious that he had left us at all. Daily, I'd see him and offer rehab. He'd gently decline with a sweetness that never grew defensive.

"Oh thanks, G, but I'm okay."

You never stop asking, and sometimes the "no matter whatness" prevails. And so it did with Pedro. I drove him to his rehab north of Los Angeles, and he began the long, hard (slow) work of returning to himself.

Thirty days into his stay there, his younger brother, Jovan, enfeebled by similar demons and displaced in the same chemical dependence, did what homies explicitly don't ever do. He put a gun to his head and an end to his pain. Homies, more often than not, just decide to put themselves in harm's way when things turn bleakest. They just take a stroll into their enemy's domain. Gangbanging is how they commit suicide. And any shooter is never "going on a mission" (foray into enemy territory) intending to kill—but rather, hoping to die. Jovan's homies were unfamiliar, then, with this new language, so direct, bypassing the slow dance with danger that eventually gets you to the same end.

I call Pedro, and he is, of course, devastated. But since he is now thirty days sober, he allows the pain passage to his core and doesn't permit the hurt to waste time, languishing in some distant way station. He lets all the sadness in, and this is new. I schedule to pick him up for the funeral and make a point to emphasize that I'll be driving him back right after the burial.

"'Course, G. I wanna come back here."

I make the trek to the mountaintop and feel inadequate, as I always do, in accompanying such loss, especially as huge as this one felt.

Emily Dickinson writes, "Hope is the thing with feathers that perches in the soul, that sings the song without the words and never stops at all."

I've come to trust the value of simply showing up—and singing the song without the words. And yet, each time I find myself sitting with the pain that folks carry, I'm overwhelmed with my own inability to do much more than stand in awe, dumbstruck by the sheer size of the burden—more than I've ever been asked to carry.

Pedro is out front waiting for me, and we greet each other with *abrazos* and a minimum of words. We hop in the car. Any worry I have about what "to say" gets punctured by Pedro's insistence to tell me about a dream he had the night before.

"It's a trip, G. I had this dream last night. And you were in it."

And in this dream, Pedro and I are in this large, empty room, just the two of us. There are no lights, no illuminated exit signs, no light creeping in from under the doors. There are no windows. There is no light. He seems to know that I am there with him. A sense, really, though we do not speak. Suddenly, in this dark silence, I retrieve a flashlight from my pocket and push it on. I find the light switch in the room, on the wall, and I shine this narrow beam of light on the switch. I don't speak. I just hold the beam steady, unwavering. Pedro says that even though no words are exchanged, he knows he is the only one who can turn this light switch on. He thanks me for happening to have a flashlight. He makes his way to the switch, following the beam with, I suppose, some trepidation. He arrives at the switch, takes a deep breath, and flips it on. The room is flooded with light.

He is now sobbing at this point, in the telling of the dream. And with a voice of astonishing discovery, he says, "And the light . . . is better . . . than the darkness."

As if he did not previously know this to be the case. He's weeping, unable to continue. Then he says, "I guess . . . my brother . . . just never found the light switch." Possessing flashlights and occasionally knowing where to aim them has to be enough for us. Fortunately, none of us can save anybody. But we all find ourselves in this dark, windowless room, fumbling for grace and flashlights. You aim the light this time, and I'll do it the next.

The slow work of God.

And you hope, and you wait, for the light—this astonishing light.

6

Jurisdiction

The walk to my office at 1916 East First Street used to take me five minutes. I'd pass Second Street School and watch parents cling to the chain-link fence, transfixed by their kids as they filed into the school building. They wouldn't leave their posts until they saw their kids walk into class. Closer to my office and before the alley was Junior's apartment. In his forties, Junior drank "forties" all day. He'd be nursing a large, cold one, even at 7:30 a.m. as I arrived to open Homeboy Industries. Most days you'd see him hanging out his window, on the second floor, shirtless, no matter the weather. He was wiry and feisty and, despite my two decades of urging "recovery" on him, alcohol didn't seem to obscure his goodness—it pickled it—it was as "out there" as his shirtless torso surveying the world from the second floor.

One day as I'm walking past, lost in my own thoughts, I fail to see him. Then after I had gone beyond his apartment and the alley, Junior screams full-throttle, "LOVE YOU G-DOG."

This stops me in my tracks as it does a few other people. I'm always startled by the ready way folks and homies tell you that they love you. This was not always so available to me in my own Irish-Catholic background. You knew people loved you, but words never brought you to that knowledge. In the barrio, people tell you. I retrace my steps and am now standing under his windowsill, looking up.

"Thank you, Junior. That was a very nice thing to say."

Junior waves me on, as if papally blessing me as my day begins.

"Oh, come on now, G, you know," he says, spinning his hand in a circular motion, "You're in my . . . jurisdiction."

I can't be entirely sure what Junior meant. Except for the fact that we all need to see that we are in each other's "jurisdictions," spheres of acceptance—only, all the time. And yet, there are lines that get drawn, and barriers erected, meant only to exclude. Allowing folks into my jurisdiction requires that I dismantle what I have set up to keep them out. Sometimes we strike the high moral distance of judgment—moving our protected jurisdictions far from each other. This is also, largely, the problem in the groupthink of gangs. They just can't seem to see one another as residing in the same jurisdiction. "We are the guys who hate those guys" is the self-defining assertion of every gang. The challenge is getting them to abandon the territory of their gang and replace it with a turf more ample, inclusive, and as expansive as God's own view of things.

In the late '80s, the gangs of the Pico-Aliso Housing Projects largely "Just Said No" to drugs. They'd sell them but didn't use them. Hard drug usage made you liable to provoke conflict with otherwise friendly gangs or, if you sold drugs, it would upset your business. One gang in particular was an exception, and PCP was its drug of choice. Members of this gang would walk up the hill to the Clock Store, an abandoned *tienda* with a looming clock stuck at a little past three. They would score their PCP—paying for "dips," dousing their cigarettes in little vials of the drug—maybe once, perhaps twice if they had the money. Then they would return to their barrio with their "kools" and get high in the safe confines of their neighborhood.

One evening, Flaco and three of his *confreres* make the trip to the Clock Store. But instead of delaying their gratification, they get high right there. This leads them to take the shortcut home—by traversing the 101 Freeway. When I get to the hospital that evening, the doctor, standing by Flaco's bed, peers down on the unconscious twenty-one-year-old and renders his verdict.

"I have never seen a body hit with such impact and still live to talk about it." This, apparently, is the good news. The bad: the car had crushed Flaco's right leg and ripped his left arm clean off his body.

I hadn't slept much that night and was decidedly, as the homies would say, "in a bad move" the next day. I was just barely getting accustomed, at that stage in my ministry, to the daily dread of disastrous things that always seem to befall those who are suspended already by the thinnest of lifelines.

I'm heading out of the church parking lot, walking toward Pico Gardens, and I see a clubhouse of gangsters congregating by the church's bell tower. This is not uncommon, as the church has become a welcoming space for them. This gang is an enemy to Flaco's gang. I walk past and greet them, and as I turn the corner, I can hear one of their group, Gato, say loudly, "I'm glad that shit happened to Flaco last night." The gathering explodes in laughter.

I double back, and I am instantly in a red-faced fury. The conventional wisdom in working with gangs would say that you never put a homie on "the front page." I do not care about this at the moment. I get in Gato's face and give him a banner headline.

"*Sabes qué, mijito.* I love you and am down for you, and I love Flaco and am down for him."

Now I am nearly nose-to-nose with Gato, and I say, "Don't you ever . . . talk that way . . . in front of me again."

This is a risky confrontation, but I am too pissed off to care.

"'*Spensa,* G," he says, in a voice ten years younger than the one he used minutes before. Some of the others chime in and share the remorse. "Sorry, G." "Come on, G, don't be mad."

Homies are good on regret, bad on restraint.

I barrel past them all and resume my march to the projects. I've had a handful of moments like this in my two decades working with homies. There were times when the futility and irrationality of the gang mind-set threw me into this frustrated place, which would occasionally play itself out like the scene above. Sometimes, you just can't think of much else to do but shake your fist and get red in the face.

The next day I'm driving out of the parking lot, and right outside is Gato. He flags me down, and I lower the window.

"Hey, G," he says. "Give me a ride, yeah? To my lady's?"

I tell him to get in and buckle up. I can feel his desire to repair what transpired the day before and am humbled at his taking the lead in this.

"Where ya goin?" he asks.

"To the hospital," I say, "to visit Flaco."

Gato says nothing. We sit in something of an icy silence. His lady lives only in Pico Gardens, so it's not much of a trip, and the silence is bearable.

When we arrive, he thanks me, shakes my hand, with the homie handshake, and opens the door to leave. He hardly makes it outside, when he sits back down.

"Do me a *paro*, G?" he says. "You tell Flaco that Gato from ___ gang says, '*Q-vo*' and that I hope he gets better."

"I will do that," I tell him, with a smile, and real admiration for the stretch this represents.

Gato makes to get out of my car again, then rapidly returns to take his seat.

"Um, G," he says, "I mean . . . don't tell my homies I said that."

I tell him that his secret is safe with me.

Sometimes you're thrown into each other's jurisdiction, and that feels better than living, as the Buddhists say, in the "illusion of separateness." It is in this place where we judge the other and feel the impossibility of anything getting bridged. The gulf too wide and the gap too distant, the walls grow higher, and we forget who we are meant to be to each other.

Somewhere, in the jurisdictional locale where judgment used to claim us, a remarkable commonality rushes in, and the barriers that exclude are dismantled.

The poet Rumi writes, "Close both eyes to see with the other eye." But finding and seeing, beyond our sense of being separate, our mutuality with the other is hard won.

Bridging the gulf of mutual judgment and replacing it with kinship is tricky indeed.

*　*　*

Chepe and Richie need to get out of town. They haven't committed a crime, but it's just a matter of time before *America's Most Wanted* comes calling. Their constant risky behavior and failure to ever be cautious has an expiration date. They are from the same gang and walking the tenuous line that separates them from bona fide trouble and innocent enough kicking it. I think they need a momentary change of venue.

I have been invited to give several talks in Bakersfield and Ridgecrest, so I snatch up Chepe and Richie for the road trip. We'll stay at my sister Maureen's house in Ridgecrest. Chepe and Richie have their own rooms and their own beds (a first), and my sister has waiting for them their own personal towels with "Richie" and "Chepe" embroidered on each.

We break up our trip with dinner at Coco's, a restaurant a notch above Denny's and a notch below, well, every place else. A very imposing woman with a missile-silo hairdo is serving as our hostess this evening. She stands behind this reception counter and glowers at the three of us—well, really, only at Chepe and Richie, shaved heads, tattooed, and in all their baggy-clothed gangster finery. I hold up three fingers to indicate the number in our party, and she budges not at all from her rock-solid, mad-dogosity. I play charades with her. Whole idea. Three people. Sit at table. Eat food. Each concept comes with its own accompanying gesture. I know exactly the origin of her displeasure, and I volley some of my own right back at her. I judge her just as surely as she judges them (barriers that exclude, all around, please). Finally, she blinks, grabs at three menus, and emerges from behind the desk, waving at us to follow her. She sighs with exasperation, not one bit happy that we have chosen Coco's for our dining pleasure. We follow the hostess's beehive through the restaurant, and let's just say we apparently are no longer in East LA. All the diners stop what they're doing, silverware suspended in midair, and a disquieting silence descends on the place. All eyes turn toward us as we move uncertainly through the divided sides of tables and customers.

Richie stage whispers, "Everybody's looking at us." I douse his concern. "Don't be ridiculous."

Everybody was looking at us.

We get to our table, in the nether bowels of the place, way beyond where the others are enjoying their meals, until we showed up.

"We don't belong here," Chepe whispers, as we settle in our booth in the projects section of Coco's. "We should go someplace else."

"What are you talkin' about?" I say, trying to dampen their paranoia.

"There's just pure, rich white people here," Richie pleads.

"Yeah," Chepe clarifies, "Them people who be eatin' Grey Poupon 'n' shit."

"Would you guys just relax. Our money is just as green as their money."

Richie excuses himself and delicately announces that he needs to "TAKE A *LEAKIAZO.*" Maybe there was one, or possibly two, people in the restaurant who actually didn't hear him broadcast where he was going. While he's gone, the waitress deposits a slew of menus—the special menu, the summer menu, the sizzling platter menu, the regular ol' menu. When Richie slinks back into the booth, he eyes this laminated array set before him and asks, "Are these 'the things'?"

"The things?" I helpfully ask.

"You know, '*the things.*'"

"The menus?"

"Oh, come on, G," Richie says with a sigh, "You knooow I don't speak 'rich.'"

This was their first time in a restaurant—where you actually sat down, a waitress came to *you,* and you didn't have to order by pointing at a luminous plastic picture of a cheeseburger.

Variations on this theme have always been bountiful. I've had homies in restaurants actually think they needed to clear the table after eating. Once a homie said, "Can I give a tip to the waitress?" and when she arrived, he said, "Just say no to drugs." His homie adding, "Don't run with scissors." The restaurant, to the gang member, is a foreign land indeed.

Our waitress is an entirely different story from the frozen and awkward reception we seem to be getting from everybody else. She puts her arms around the "fellas," calling Chepe and Richie "Sweetie" and "Honey" and bringing them refills ("and we didn't even have to ask"), with extra this and more of that, and supplying the Tapatío on demand. She is Jesus in an apron.

Later, as we walk to the car, they talk about our waitress. "She was *firme.*"

"Yeah, she treated us like we were somebody."

We have a chance, sometimes, to create a new jurisdiction, a place of astonishing mutuality, whenever we close both eyes of judgment and open the other eye to pay attention. Reminding each other how acceptable we are and lavishly providing free refills and all the Tapatío you need. Suddenly, we find ourselves in the same room with each other and the walls are gone.

One of the great fonts of sadness in the prison system and the Youth Authority in California is the heightened division between the races. At the reception center of the Youth Authority in Norwalk (SRCC), once a month I celebrate two Masses back-to-back in a multipurpose center.

At roughly 6 p.m. and 7 p.m. on a Sunday, the wards are brought in and sit on metal folding chairs. They are almost all Latino. In the early days, my helpers, those who set up for Mass and did the readings, were Jerome (African American), Larry (Caucasian), and Juan (Latino). They were great friends, and their bond seemed to jar, somewhat, the racial boundaries so tightly held in these places. When I first arrived there, they schooled me on my responsibilities and seemed to confuse my first Mass at SRCC with "my first Mass ever."

"We will have the Offertory." Larry explains as if (as the homies say) this was "my first barbeque."

Juan picks up: "The Offertory is when we bring you the gifts." Juan enunciates like I'm not a native speaker—in any language. "The gifts,"—Jerome brings us home—"are the bread and the wine."

I'm acting as if I'm taking mental notes, *Hmmm . . . bread . . . wine . . . tell me more.*

"And then," Jerome says, proceeding, "I will come over with a bowl, and I will pour water over your fingers."

He leans in, furtively, and manages a whisper, "so, you know . . . you can wash your iniquities."

I told him I was able to scrub the heck out of my iniquities before I got there. But thanks anyway.

Once before Mass, the Catholic chaplain, Tom Moletaire, tells me that Juan is going to sing a solo after communion. We had never had singing in all my time coming to this place, and I congratulate Juan before the Mass begins. The moment arrives, and Juan steps up to the microphone and begins to sing a cappella.

It's jaw-droppingly bad. What comes from this kid's pipes is some vague sound of small-animal torture. We are all stunned. I quickly check the faces of the couple hundred wards sitting there. They can be, shall we say, a tough bunch. They are agog, and the singing is so bad that the part of their brains that handles laughter doesn't get the message in time. They stare flabbergasted. The first Mass ends, and I find myself assiduously avoiding any contact with Juan. I do not have a clue what words to put together on his postcommunion *canción*.

Soon enough, the seats are filled again, and Mass number two is launched. Now, I just presume Juan won't attempt this a second time. But sure enough, communion ends, and Juan steps up to the microphone with seemingly no lack of confidence. And he accomplishes something I would not have thought possible. It is worse than the first time around. It is an outtake from *American Idol*. Again, no catcalls or giggles, not even shifting in seats. The congregation is frozen comatose in the sheer awfulness of it. Now, after this Mass, there is no avoiding it; I have to say something to Juan without failing the lie-detector test.

"Juan," I say, with my hand on his shoulder and Larry and Jerome closing the circle around him, "You know, uh, it takes a lot of courage to READ in front of people, but it takes EVEN MORE courage to get up and SING in front of people."

Then Jerome steps up and places his arm over Juan's shoulder. "And it takes EVEN MORE courage to get up and sing . . . when yo ass can't sing."

In an instant, I'm preparing myself to break up a fight. But just as quickly, the three of them have a meltdown of laughter, and soon they are on the floor of this multipurpose center, convulsing and smacking each other. We seek to create loving communities of kinship precisely to counteract mounting lovelessness, racism, and the cultural disparagement that keeps us apart.

* * *

In the spring of 1993, when I am in tertianship, I find myself on a prison island in the Pacific Ocean off Mexico. Islas Marias, Mexico's "Alcatraz," is a twelve-hour barge ride from Mazatlán. The Jesuits celebrate fifty years of service there during my three-month stay. I live by myself (sleeping on a mattress in the sacristy of a small chapel) in a remote part of the island called Camp Bugambilias, where nearly eight hundred *colonos* (inmates) make bricks, tend livestock, and do a variety of other tasks of manual labor. Men are allowed to live with their families in simple bungalows, but the vast majority of the imprisoned are single men who live in dilapidated dorms. I make bricks with them all morning long, have Mass in the afternoon, and play dominoes at night. We even put on quite an elaborate Passion Play during my brief stay. I eat with the *colonos,* and the food is unspeakably bad, right out of the Dickens cookbook. "Gruel" does not do justice to what they slop on our plates. I lose forty pounds.

At brickmaking one morning (which, by the way, means we play in the mud, pour the stuff into wood slats, let it bake in the sun, then stack these *tabique* high to build walls), Beto, a daily mudslinger with me, tells me to meet him at noon at the lieutenant's garden.

"Bring your backpack" should have been my first clue that we are headed for trouble. Beto is *tremendo:* mischievous, funny, in his midthirties, always longing to dance right near the ledge of danger and dangle himself there in defiance of all reason. I have already seen him run afoul of the lieutenant, an exacting and spectacularly mean man, who runs Camp Bugambilias. Beto, by the way, was excellent as Peter in our Passion Play.

I meet Beto as planned, standing with my backpack (like a *menso*, I might add) outside the lieutenant's home. He has a flourishing vegetable garden filled with all the things none of us had tasted in a very long time. Beto arrives, says, "Wait here," and kangaroos himself over the garden fence. Before I can get out "What the hell are you doing?" Beto is snatching up carrots and tomatoes, peppers and lettuce. He's holding his T-shirt stretched in front of him, hopping down the aisles of the garden, tossing in zucchini, eggplant, and a couple of lemons for good measure. I'm in a panic. I have heard often of what passes as punishment in the camp.

If a *colono,* for example, "escapes" to the mountains (leaving the island is unthinkable—too many sharks), the entire camp is given even worse food until they capture the inmate, who is carried into camp, tied on a stick, hanging from legs and hands like an iguana, and is soundly beaten. I never witnessed any of this— but the stories are numerous. I only see the lieutenant's constant yelling and public humiliation of the *colonos.*

I am doing some involuntary jig outside the fence, looking in all directions and whining quietly, "Hurry, hurry." Beto leaps over to my side of the fence, looking seven months pregnant, takes my backpack (thank you very much), and fills it with the purloined produce. "Let's go," he says, and hightail it we do. We run like crazy people to a spot Beto has set up a bit north of the dorm and secluded enough among the trees and the brush. He has a pot and starts a fire. He's been carrying a cloth sack that seems to have a life of its own. This is due, entirely, to the presence of a very large, live iguana rustling inside. Catching iguanas is also strictly forbidden and punishable by beating with a very large stick. Beto guts the iguana, and it begins to simmer in the pot (and, yes, it tastes just like chicken).

I watch as he dexterously wields his knife around the carrots and slices and dices the other vegetables. I help where I can, stirring the concoction, but mainly staying out of Beto's way. He knows what he's doing. I admire his earnestness and the care with which he prepares our *caldo de iguana*. The aroma nearly brings tears to our eyes. I haven't smelled something so savory and delectable in a long time. It is longer still for Beto.

As the smoke from lunch makes its way beyond the trees, we begin to receive visitors. A *colono* shows up and asks what we're up to. I watch Beto to see how he'll treat the intrusion. He tells the old man, "We're making *caldo de iguana*. Join us."

I'm moved by the ease with which Beto lets this guy in and smoothly adds some water to the pot. The man tells us that he has something back in the dorm, and in short order he appears again with a small ball of crumbled old newspaper. He peels it open and there is a clump of coarse salt he had been saving for just the right moment. Beto tosses it in. Shortly another uninvited *colono* shows up, and Beto adds again to the simmering pot some accommodating water and more vegetables. This inmate does the same retrieval of the safely guarded ingredient back in the dorm. This time it's a slightly shriveled jalapeno pepper. It's diced and added to the mix. Another arrives, same inclusion, same retrieval. This guy has a rusted, small can of tomato paste. Once they figure out how to open it, it, too, goes in.

Maybe there are eight of us or so when the meal finally gets served. Plenty to go around and just as tasty as it could be. Everyone brought his flavor to this forbidden pot of iguana stew, and keeping anyone away and excluded was unthinkable to this band of prisoners. Alone, they didn't have much, but together, they had a potful of plenty.

* * *

No question gets asked of me more than, "What's it like to have enemies working together?"

The answer: it is almost always tense at first. A homie will beg for a job, and perhaps I have an opening at the Bakery.

"But you're gonna have to work with X, Y, and Z," naming enemies already working there. He thinks a bit and invariably will say: "I'll work with him, but I'm not gonna talk to him."

In the early days, this would unsettle me. Until I discovered that it always becomes impossible to demonize someone you know.

* * *

I take two recently hired enemies, Artie and Danny, to Oakland for a talk I'm to give. They will man the table in the front and sell Homeboy and Homegirl merchandise. The trip is excruciating as they will not speak to each other. I carry the ball entirely in the conversation and only occasionally do they grunt assent or nod, "uh-huh."

Before the talk, we're standing on the terrace at our hotel, overlooking a boardwalk along the water, near Jack London Square in Oakland. We stand there in silence watching the people below. I give up trying to keep things conversational.

Down below, there is a sweet old couple, probably married well beyond fifty years. They are holding hands. Danny elbows Artie and points at the old couple. "That's disgusting."

"*Cómo que* 'disgusting'?" I turn on him. "It's sweet. It's an old couple."

"Still," Danny says, "it's disgusting."

"What are you talking about?" I press him.

"Well, it's only obvious." Danny points one more time as the couple disappear from sight. "They're under the influence of Viagra."

A completely silly joke by anyone's standards, but Artie and Danny collapse in howling and high fives.

Some passage has been cleared, and they both choose to move through it. An artificially silly wall has divided them, only to be brought to rubble by an outrageously silly thing.

A footnote: Artie and Danny become great and enduring friends, whose friendship has to be kept secret always from their own homeboys.

Thomas Merton writes, "We discover our true selves in love." Nothing is more true than this in Artie and Danny. Love never fails. It will always find a way to have its way.

Before Homeboy Industries grew too huge, I used to walk new hires to their job site and introduce them to their coworkers.

"Clever" seems eager to begin at Homeboy Silkscreen, and at twenty-two years old, he has assured me, he is ready to retire his jersey from the barrio. He moves with me easily through the factory, shaking hands cheerfully with those printing shirts or catching them as they are spit through the conveyor-belt dryer. Even enemies he greets and looks them in the eye.

Until he turns a corner and sees Travieso, a twenty-four-year-old from an enemy hood. In unison, they stare instantly at their feet, some mumbling takes place, and there is a great mutual shifting of body weight. They do not shake hands. I think, *Hell, he's just finished shaking hands with all sorts of enemies.*

I discover, sometime later, that the hatred they hold for each other is *profundo*. Not only is this a neighborhood *pedo*, this is also personal. Some *delito* has transpired between them, and the breach is beyond repair. I can sense this much in the moment, even before the details get filled in later.

Their eyes are still epoxied to their Nike Cortezes. "Look," I tell them, "if you can't hang working together—please let me know now. I gotta grip a' homies who would love to have this *jale*." They say nothing, so that's that.

Some six months later, Travieso finds himself surrounded in an alley, greatly outnumbered by members of an enemy gang who beat him badly. While he is lying there, they will not stop kicking his head until he is still and lifeless, and then they leave him. Someone gets him to White Memorial Hospital where he is declared brain dead and left on life support. The doctors wait for forty-eight hours to secure a flat read, and then they can officially declare him deceased. This allows time for relatives to journey to Los Angeles.

I am speaking at St. Louis University and fly home. I have seen a great deal of horrifying things in my lifetime—nothing, however, compares to the sight of this kid (a wonderfully, gentle-souled kid) with his head swollen many times its size. It is breath-taking. I can barely keep my eyes trained on him as I smear sacred oil on his forehead and we say good-bye in the pull of a plug.

In those first twenty-four hours after his death, I am in my office, late at night, and the phone rings. It's Clever.

"Hey," he begins awkwardly, "that's messed up . . . 'bout what . . . happened to Travieso."

"Yeah, it is," I say to him, brought back to this hollow area of my soul, which this sadness has carved.

"Is there anything I can do?" Clever asks, with oddly high energy, "Can I give him my blood?"

This last offer sucks the breathable air out of the atmosphere for both of us. We can each feel the other tremble in silence. Clever takes the lead and punctures the quiet, with great resolve and unprotected tears.

"He . . . was . . . not . . . my . . . enemy. He was my friend. We . . . worked together."

*　　*　　*

Close both eyes; see with the other one. Then, we are no longer saddled by the burden of our persistent judgments, our ceaseless withholding, our constant exclusion. Our sphere has widened, and we find ourselves, quite unexpectedly, in a new, expansive location, in a place of endless acceptance and infinite love.

We've wandered into God's own "jurisdiction."

7

Gladness

What the American poet William Carlos Williams said of poetry could well be applied to the living of our lives: "If it ain't a pleasure, it ain't a poem." My director of novices, Leo Rock, used to say, "God created us—because He thought we'd enjoy it."

We try to find a way, then, to hold our fingertips gently to the pulse of God. We watch as our hearts begin to beat as one with the One who delights in our being. Then what do we do? We exhale that same spirit of delight into the world and hope for poetry.

I remember being invited to an early-morning radio show, in Spanish. It's in-studio and covers nearly two hours of the drive to work, 7 to 9 a.m. Callers ask me about gangs, and, often enough, mothers seek advice about their wayward children. *"Tenemos una llamada de Yolanda, de Inglewood."* It goes on like this for some time. As we near the nine o'clock hour, they take another call. *"Tenemos una llamada de Filiberto, de Downey."*

I think—*Filiberto is not that common a name, and I have a worker named Fili who also lives in Downey.* The voice booms into the studio.

"Hey, yeah, G, it's me, Fili . . . Yeah . . . well, I'm not feelin' so good . . . so I'm just callin' to let ya know—I won't be coming into work today."

Fili has chosen a radio call-in show to call in sick.

"Um . . . okay . . . Fili," I say, stunned. "Uh, hope you feel better."

As I drive home after the show, replaying Fili's call over and over in my head, I steep in the utter fullness of not wanting to have anyone else's life but my own.

(In the category of "Can You Top This?"—a homie supplies an excuse to Norma Gillette, who has worked at Homeboy longer than anybody and consequently has heard it all: the homie says to her, "I have Anal Blindness."

"Anal Blindness?" she says.

"Yeah, I just can't see my ass coming to work today.")

Apparently, FDR had a sign on his desk that read: "Let unconquerable gladness dwell." Our search to know what's on God's mind ends in the discovery of this same unconquerable gladness.

Dorothy Day loved to quote Ruskin, who urged us all to the "Duty to Delight." It was an admonition, really, to be watchful for the hilarious and the heartwarming, the silly and the sublime. This way will not pass again, and so there is a duty to be mindful of that which delights and keeps joy at the center, distilled from all that happens to us in a day.

Nearly eight o'clock at night, I pass the front of the emergency room at White Memorial Hospital. On the bus bench, all by himself, is Spider. He's wearing pastel blue scrubs, and he's just gotten off work. He is a light-skinned *huero*, and his hair rests in the limbo between clean-shaven *pelón* and locks ready to be trained by a dollop of Three Flowers. It is all tucked neatly under a nylon stocking.

I had only met him recently and come to know his story. He isn't nineteen yet and works in the hospital as an orderly, moving patients and equipment, a job he secured through Homeboy Industries. Spider is from a gang in Aliso Village, where he and his sister mainly raised themselves, having been abandoned by their parents. I was never quite sure how they duped the Housing Authority into thinking there was a responsible adult around. He and his lady, with two small sons, now live in an apartment in Highland Park, several bus rides away.

"Get in, dog, I'll take ya home."

We speak of many things as we go, and I question him about his bills and rent and how he's faring. I've helped him get jump-started in this regard a few times already.

"I'm okay," he says, then steers himself in a whole other direction. "You know what I'm gonna do when I get home right now? I'm gonna sit down to eat with my lady and my two *morritos*. But, well . . . I don't eat. I just watch them eat. My lady she gets crazy with me, but I don't care. I just watch 'em eat. They eat and eat. And I just look at 'em and thank God they're in my life. When they're done eating and I know they're full, THEN I eat.

"And the truth . . . sometimes there's food left and sometimes there isn't. *Tú sabes*," he says to me, putting his hand on my shoulder as I drive, "it's a Father thing." The duty to delight is to stare at your family as they eat, anchored in the surest kind of gratitude—the sort that erases sacrifice and hardship and absorbs everything else. Jesus says, "My ways are not your ways," but they sure could be. In the utter simplicity of breathing, we find how naturally inclined we are to delight and to stay dedicated to gladness. We bask in God's unalloyed joy, and we let loose with that same joy in whoever is in front of us. We forget what a vital part of our nature this is.

*   *   *

From diagnosis of a brain tumor to his death, my father lasted thirty days. We had noticed at the dinner table, when many of us were home one weekend, that one side of Dad's face was droopy. Soon he was at St. Vincent's Hospital for tests. He spent a handful of nights there, separated from my mother, a rare occurrence in their forty-eight years of marriage. On one of those initial days, I go to retrieve my mom at her home. As I wait in the driveway, she emerges from the house, arms laden with magazines and bags and an elongated pillow with a flowery case. I help her with the things and then try to help her with my commentary. "You know, St. Vincent's provides pillows." She makes a face and sighs heavily. "Oh gosh . . . your father . . . he asked for a pillow from MY side of the bed." We eye-roll our way into the car.

At the hospital, my folks greet each other in their customary way—the two-peck kiss. Two birds snatching up the last seeds. My mom slides into the restroom, and I am at the window of his room, just north of the head of his bed. I'm about to make small talk about the view from up here, but I turn and see that my father has placed the flowery pillow over his face. He breathes in so deeply and then exhales, as he places the pillow behind his head. For the rest of the morning, I catch him turning and savoring again the scent of the woman whose bed he's shared for nearly half a century. We breathe in the spirit that delights in our being—the fragrance of it. And it works on us. Then we exhale (for that breath has to go somewhere)—to breathe into the world this same spirit of delight, confident that this is God's only agenda.

We want to cover our bets, though. A battle gets waged between disparate takes on God's hidden agenda. What seems to vex us is our tendency to conjure up a tiny God. I remember arriving at a CEB (base community) meeting in my very earliest days at Dolores Mission. Spanish, in those days, was more of a struggle than it is now. When I arrive, an older lady, Lupe, strong and influential in the group, has gotten her hands on this tiny brochure. It's a message from the Blessed Mother, and, boy, is Mary pissed! There apparently was an apparition somewhere in New Jersey. A woman is *calientando* a tortilla, and when she flips it over, *Ay, Dios Mio!* there is an image of La Virgin in all her glory. So apart from imminent plans to build a cathedral, say, right in this kitchen, Mary has come with a message. This little brochure explains it all. So Lupe is holding us hostage and has completely derailed our meeting. Mary is gonna let us have it, she tells us, and she is not one bit pleased with the state of the world, and everybody is going to hell on the "Dynamite D" train. This is the gist. I feel hopeless to bring us back on track, no match for the fluidity and command of Lupe. She has us in her thrall for some time, until Socorro, a respected and elderly "church lady," a sacristan and gentle soul, *pidio la palabra*. She daintily poises her finger in the air, asking to be heard. The only power I have in the group, at this point, is to permit her to speak.

"Well, you know," Socorro begins with a quiet strength and humble tone, "I am from a ranchito in Mexico. I've never been to school. I can't read the Bible. I certainly can't read that fine *folleto* you've brought to our meeting, Lupe." Then she pauses as if to employ some other unseen second engine. She gears up and rears up and looks straight at Lupe. *"Pero, te digo una cosa, Dios no es así."* (I'll tell ya one thing, God is not like that.)

Socorro knew the opposite of God when she saw it. God is surely too busy delighting in us to want to ship us off in handbaskets to Hades. Socorro knew this with unshakeable certainty (and with, I might add, a dash of unconquerable gladness).

Socorro finds herself, as Bill Cain says, "living within the withinness of God." This is the intimate union and full promise of kinship that is being offered to us every second. The poet Hafez writes, "We are content with a phantom of you. Oh God, how pitifully poor our aspirations are. And how estranged and distant, how far we are from union!" It is okay to aspire to a glad and delighting union offered every moment, right here, right now. Woody Allen says, "I'm not afraid of death, I just don't want to be there when it happens." Everything on this side of death, however, is "requesting the honor of our presence" so we can delight in life's astonishing, joyful poetry.

*   *   *

Moreno now works at the reception center in our brand-new headquarters. In his midtwenties, he is the father of two daughters and has worked at Homeboy for six years. I have watched him grow immeasurably into a responsible, mature worker. (If there is an area for further growth, it's in his language. I'm always trying to curb his tendency to the *mal hablado*. He's trying too.

He left me a voice message not long ago: "Hey, G, yeah, it's me, Moreno, 'n shit . . . I mean, *'spensa,* it's me, Moreno and FECES." I think we can all agree—progress.) He was a tiny, skinny kid when I met him years ago through some of his homies. An elementary school dropout, he was getting socialized on the streets. His mom couldn't keep him at home or in school, and he had a disaffected relationship with his stepfather. He was a kid classically unable to find a strain of enthusiasm in his life. Delighting was some foreign country, say, Mozambique. He always made a point of letting you know that he was entirely "too cool" to get excited by much. I call him once and ask what he's doing. "Just right here—blaséing it." As an English major, I was actually not aware you could do that to "blasé."

Street life finally catches up with Moreno, and he gets locked up. After the briefest of stints in Juvenile Hall, he gets sent to a "suitable placement" instead of a probation camp. Days after arriving at this group home in Orange County, he is enrolled in the local high school, and two weeks into school, he calls me. "Hey, G, kidnap me, yeah? I don't got no clothes and, *tú sabes, mi jefita,* she don't got no ends. So, yeah? Kidnap me?" Moreno was aware that at Homeboy we had a program called "New Image," which allows us to buy clothes for gang members released from detention facilities—enabling them to trade in their oversize Ben Davis for Dockers that *más o menos* fit them. I arrange with the group home staff to "kidnap" Moreno on the upcoming Saturday.

I pick up Moreno, and it is immediately apparent that, today, he's decided to stand tall for the "Blaséing-It Movement." No matter what I say, I can't topple him from his "whatever" parapet.

Naturally, I press him on school. "Wow, dog—I mean, *felicidades*. Nice goin', you're in school again after all these years. So, how's it feel?"

Moreno shrugs—can't even muster a "whatever."

"Now, come on, son, you gotta have a favorite subject?"

"Nope."

"How 'bout English?"

"Hate it."

"Math?"

"The worst."

"Like History?"

"Can't stand it."

"There's gotta be sumthin' ya like . . . Do you . . . have a science?"

These last words of mine seem to have a cattle prod attached to them. Were it not for the seat belt, he'd be in my lap.

"DAMN, G—BIOOOOLOGY. THAT'S THE BOOOOOMB, right there." He settles in to have me share his joy. "Watcha, dog," he continues, "On Monday, we're gonna DIGEST a frog!"

I nearly swerve into oncoming traffic.

Greatly amused, I say to him, "Well, actually, *mijo*, it's not *digest* a frog, it's *dissect* a frog."

Moreno resumes the blasé.

"Yeah, well, whatever . . . Monday we're fuckin' with a frog."

The poet Mary Oliver writes, "All things are inventions of holiness—some more rascally than others." There is magical poetry in a kid on the margins discovering biology. Moreno is all the more holy in being "rascally" about it.

Some time back, at the turn of the century, during a general election, some pundit tried to compare and contrast Bill Clinton, Al Gore, and George W. Bush. He said Bill Clinton walks into a room and wants everybody in the room to like him. Al Gore walks into a room and wants everyone to thinks he's right. "W" walks into a room and wants the room to know he's in charge. We all feel all of these at one time or another, because they're fear-based responses, and it's hard to get out from under that dread. Our frightened selves want only for the gathered to like us, to agree with us, or be intimidated by us. I suppose Jesus walks into a room and loves what he finds there. Delights in it, in fact. Maybe, He makes a beeline to the outcasts and chooses, in them, to go where love has not yet arrived. His ways aren't our ways, but they sure could be.

We have grown accustomed to think that loving as God does is hard. We think it's about moral strain and obligation. We presume it requires a spiritual muscularity of which we are not capable, a layering of burden on top of sacrifice, with a side order of guilt. (But it was love, after all, that made the cross salvific, not the sheer torture of it.)

I've been keeping informal track of "homie-propisms" at all the detention facilities where I celebrate the Eucharist. These are the moments when the homies get up to read and they'll come to an unfamiliar word and will supplant it with one they know rather than what it should be. Sometimes, it's the usual slipup. "A reading from the letter of Paul to the Phillipinos." They don't know what a Gentile is but have a passing familiarity with "Genitals." (Try this one yourself—go to the Acts of the Apostles and substitute "genitals" wherever you find "Gentiles." It livens up this book as never before.) Psalm 23 gets read as "Beside resentful waters, he leads me." Resentment they know, rest is what they could use more of.

Homie-propisms aren't limited to liturgical celebrations. A homie called me once, experiencing hard economic times: "It's so bad, I had to go eat at the Starvation Army." Once, a homie needed legal assistance: "Hey, G, ya think you could get me a lawyer for free. You know, one who'll do the legal work, Sonny Bono." A homie in the office wrote a phone message: "Professor Davis at UC Irvine wants you to give a talk. YOU WILL BE CON-STIPATED." I went to the homie, who apparently had powers to predict my future, and was relieved to discover that I would be "compensated." Whew.

The Suffering Servant passage from Isaiah is proclaimed: "He did not shield his face from buffets"—not pronounced as it should be, like Warren and Jimmy's last name, but as in Home-town—all you can eat. (I remember first hearing it this way, and as one who rarely shields his face from any buffet—I felt thoroughly indicted.) My favorite homie-propism happened at the Dorothy Kirby Center, a locked-down placement for juvenile males and females. An African American sixteen-year-old boy arrives early at the tiny Kirby chapel and wants to practice his reading before Mass. It is the Responsorial Psalm, whose refrain is, "The Lord is my shepherd. There is nothing I shall want." His voice fills the chapel, and he is positively stentorian. Olivier. It is great. He moves through the psalm with an absence of self-consciousness, reading the verses and then indicating (with a sweeping hand gesture) to the congregation, which isn't there yet, when they are to chime in with him: "The Lord is my shepherd. There is nothing I shall want." Soon, both sides of the aisles fill, and Mass begins. Our man approaches to lead us in the responsorial psalm. There is something about him that makes me watch carefully. Nerves haven't kicked in—quite the opposite. He is cocky and acts as if he's requested the net to be removed. He seems to want to maximize eye contact. He figures he's practiced enough—got the thing memorized. And so he makes the exaggerated movement with his hand and leads our little congregation: "Our response to the psalm this evening is: "The Lord . . . is nothing I shall want." The volunteers, in unison, cringe and scramble with their body language to find some way to push this toothpaste back into its container. Too late. The congregation belts back to our leader, "THE LORD IS NOTHING I SHALL WANT."

There is enough strained obligation in what we think God asks of us that our mantra might as well be "The Lord is nothing I shall want." But the task at hand is only about delighting—with joy at the center. At ease. We can all relax. John 3:16 is displayed on big signs at every televised sporting event. "Yes, God so loved the world . . ." Yet the most electrifying, wholly affirming, life-altering word in the entire sentence is "Yes." It's about alignment with God's own "yes," deciding to actually be there, all the time, when delight happens. So, as the letter of James ends, "Let your yes mean yes."

* * *

One day, I'm looking for a runner—a homie to take a message to someone else in the building. I look up from my desk and see two homies in the "well" (the sunken computer area in the old office, where phones got answered and data entry got entered). I spot Mario and Frankie, two big homies, staring at a computer screen intently "working" (though "work" may be too strong a word). I'm about to call Frankie to be my runner, when I observe him lean into Mario's chest and take a deep, deep breath. He exhales contentedly.

"Frankie, come here a minute," I yell at him from my office inner sanctum. He looks cookie-jar startled. Embarrassed, he runs to my office. I hand him the message and instruct him to go to the financial office. He inches toward the door to leave but then turns around, sheepish and tentative.

"Uh, G . . . uh, did you see me . . . right now . . . you know . . . smelling Mario?"

I admit that I had.

"Damn," Frankie huffs and puffs, "I mean, it's just that . . . well . . . he be smellin' GOOOOD. I mean . . . all the homies . . . we be likin' his cologne." Breathe it in, breathe it out. The Lord is everything I want. A yes that means yes. You want to be there when the poetry happens. Isaiah has God say: "Be glad forever and rejoice in what I create . . . for I create my people to be a delight." God thinking we'd enjoy ourselves. Delighting is what occupies God, and God's hope is that we join in. That God's joy may be in us and this joy may be complete. We just happen to be God's joy. That takes some getting used to.

*　*　*

Leon Dufour, a world-renowned Jesuit theologian and Scripture scholar, a year before he died at ninety-nine, confided in a Jesuit who was caring for him, "I have written so many books on God, but after all that, what do I really know? I think, in the end, God is the person you're talking to, the one right in front of you." A mantra I use often, to keep me focused in delight on the person in front of me, comes from an unlikely place. I find it in Jesus' words to the good *ladrón* nailed next to him. He essentially says, "This day . . . with me . . . Paradise." It's not just a promise of things to come; it is a promise for the here and now . . . with Him . . . on this day, in fact . . . Paradise.

Thich Nhat Hahn writes that "our true home is the present moment, the miracle is not to walk on water. The miracle is to walk on the green earth in the present moment." The ancient Desert Fathers, when they were disconsolate and without hope, would repeat one word, over and over, as a kind of soothing mantra. And the word wasn't "Jesus" or "God" or "Love." The word was "Today." It kept them where they needed to be.

I come back from a speaking trip, and Marcos is sitting there in the reception area. Gus at the front desk tells me, "He's been waiting for ya, for like three days." Marcos greets me and is brimming with news. "While you were gone—my son was born."

"Nice goin', *mijo*—tell, me, when was he born?"

"ON HIS BIRTHDAY!" (*Wow,* I think, *what are the chances of that happening!*)

God, right there, today, in the person in front of me, joy beyond holding, beholding this day, Paradise. You delight in what is before you today in Christ. Richard Rolheiser writes that, "the opposite of depression is not happiness, it's delight." After all, we breathe the Spirit that delights in our being. We don't breathe in the Spirit that just sort of puts up with our mess. It's about delight.

Before they tore down the projects of Pico Gardens and then rebuilt them, the two identifying locales within them were "first and second playgrounds." They were areas ostensibly for kids to play in, though the jungle gyms looked like hand-me-downs from Mogadishu, and the patch of lawn never deepened in color past yellow. "Meet you at second playground" was commonly heard, or "They crept in at first playground and started blasting" was also (*desafortunadamente*) a recurring refrain.

On a summer night, I'm on my bike and settle in the heart of second playground. It's still light out, and soon I'm surrounded by homies from this barrio. I straddle the bike and listen to the homies "bagging" on one another (kidding one another endlessly—truth be told, this is the main occupation of all gang members). There are eight who ultimately gather here, the banter is fast, and no prisoners are taken. In a flash, one of the homies, Minor (a "new booty"), points up to a telephone wire perched above the apartments (each playground is surrounded by two-story apartments, boxing the play areas into squares).

"Look, G, IT'S AN OWL."

"YEAH, DAMN, A FUCKIN' OWL," says another.

"In the projects," a third chimes in, setting our collective volume to a hush, indicating that some cathedral has just been entered. Sure enough, there is the largest owl imaginable resting on this telephone wire just above Lupe Loera's *cantón*. We stand in a straight line, eyeing this anomalous creature that has chosen to visit the poorest, most owl-less sector in LA (pigeons and mice are generally our only wildlife). Mouths agape, the silence is maintained only briefly as Psycho turns to Minor with a whisper.

"Get the gauge."

"Nope," Gonzo intervenes, reaching over and touching Minor on the arm. As a shot-caller, Gonzo's "got it like that."

"No," Gonzo says, with the heft of some tribal leader. "Let him be." No one wants to speak too loudly or make any sudden moves. Even when it does occur to someone in the group to say something, no one takes his eyes off this bird.

"It's a sign," says one.

"From God," adds another.

"What's it mean, G?" says Minor, the wide-eyed pup of this litter.

I lean in to him, but with a stage whisper so all can hear. "It's God saying to give up your weapons, love your enemies, and work for peace." The unified moan nearly sends our unexpected owl packing.

"You think every sign means that?" (Uh-oh. Gonzo's onto me.)

There we stand as others join our vigil in the temple worship of this massive animal. Silence prevails, as no church service I've seen ever commands, until this astonishing owl opens its wings and takes off (suspecting, no doubt, that Psycho and his gauge can't be restrained forever). And he is gone in a majestic flapping and a slow-motion gliding, disappearing from view behind the gigantic tower of the corn factory fronting the projects. Today. This day. An owl. Second playground. Together we breathe this all in, and it seems a paradise to us.

* * *

I take Israel and Tony with me to Christ the King parish in Los Angeles. I'm going to speak after the parish spaghetti feed and my two associates will try to sell out all the Homeboy/Homegirl merchandise we've packed in our trunk. But first, they have to sit through the 5:30 p.m. Saturday Mass, with me presiding. On the way home that night, Tony, singularly impressed at Israel's breadth of liturgical knowledge, regales me. Apparently, Israel had absolutely nailed all the responses.

"May the Lord be with you."

"And also with you," Israel confidently returns.

"Lift up your hearts."

"We lift them up to the Lord." No beat gets missed in Israel's comeback. Tony stares at him, amazed. This goes on for the duration of the Mass, and Tony keeps turning and marveling at Israel's adroit certainty in this back and forth of liturgical protocol.

"Let us proclaim the mystery of faith."

And Israel, blindfolded and hands tied behind his back, returns the volley.

"Christ has died. Christ is risen. Christ will come again."

That does it. Tony can't take it anymore.

"Hey," he says, tilting toward Israel and whispering, "How you know all this?"

"Juvenile Hall, fool."

If only Tony had been detained on as many cases as Israel, he, too, would be churchgoer of the year.

As we bask in God's attention, our eyes adjust to the light, and we begin to see as God does. Then, quite unexpectedly, we discover what Mary Oliver calls "the music with nothing playing."

It is an essential tenet of Buddhism that we can begin to change the world by first changing how we look at the world. The Vatican II Council Fathers simply decided to change the opening words of their groundbreaking encyclical, "Gaudium et Spes." Originally, it read, speaking of the world: "The grief and the anguish . . ." Then they just decided to cross out those words and famously inserted instead, "The joy and the hope . . ." No new data had rushed in on them, and the world hadn't changed suddenly. They just chose, in a heartbeat, to see the world differently. They hadn't embraced, all of a sudden, Pollyannaism. They had just put on a whole new set of eyewear.

One of my favorite examples of this came from a sixteen-year-old homie and, no doubt, budding Buddhist, Lorenzo. He settled into a chair in front of my desk, and when I looked up, I saw he had scratches all over his face, and his two forearms were raspberried with scrapes. He was pretty much beat up, and I presumed an encounter with rivals.

"My God," I say to him, "What happened to you?"

Lorenzo, nonchalant and unbothered, points at his numerous red markings and scabs and dismisses it all with glee.

"Oh this? My bike was teaching me how to fly." Music with nothing playing.

* * *

On an early Saturday morning, several members of an enemy gang, with faces obscured in ski masks, enter a part of the projects where they are certain to catch some rivals "slippin'." They turn a corner and see three brothers enjoying the bright early-morning sun right outside their kitchen door. Clearly, the older two, Rickie and Adam, twenty and eighteen, are targets for the invading masked men, but in the frenzy of bullets flying, their twelve-year-old brother, Jacob, not from any gang, is felled, and his brothers' lives are altered immeasurably and forever.

I had known this family since 1984 and watched how, almost imperceptibly, the older brothers would dance close to the gang life and then drift back to other, safer boundaries. Eventually, they were in, and the death of their baby brother, from a bullet inscribed with other names, would be their pervasive and enduring wound for some time to come.

I hired them both shortly after their brother was killed, and they worked in our Homeboy Merchandising division, selling T-shirts, mugs, mouse pads, and a variety of items sporting the Homeboy logo. They worked closely with enemies—even those who belonged to the gang surely responsible for their brother's death.

A speaking gig to San Francisco came up, and I invited them both—thinking a change of scenery would restore them. They were very excited but completely confounded to discover (once we were at the airport) that, well, we were going to fly and not drive. I guess I thought I had made this clear. Seeing their panic, I decide not to calm them down. Instead, I stop under the wing of the Southwest Airlines plane (at Burbank Airport you walk the tarmac and climb the steps) and stare up, with consternation. "Uh-oh," I say as they rush to my side in a breathless "What?" "What?" unison. I point. "I don't know—is that a crack in the wing, or am I seeing things?" It takes them a while to see what I'm doing, and then they say in brotherly chorus, "You ain't right," "Damn, don't be doing that."

We climb the stairs and find our seats. Rickie lets his younger brother, Adam, get "SHOTGUN" (which I suggest is usually not a thing one tends to yell on planes nowadays). Quickly they discover the laminated emergency cards in the pouch before them, and Adam thinks they're menus and that we're in a flying Denny's. "Two oxygens, please, when you get a chance," he says to the "waitress," who fortunately for all involved does not actually hear him. The pilot speaks over the intercom and drones on in his pilot cadence, "We'll be traveling at an altitude of, etc . . .

thank you for flying Southwest Airlines." I shake my head with some force. "Damn, I hate that." Again, they turn and begin the "What?" "What?" refrain. "Well," I tell them, "It's ten a.m., and I think our pilot has had a couple of 40s already," making tippling gestures with my hand. "OK . . . cut . . . that . . . out." They seem to be catching on more quickly now.

"Well, what I want to know is, where's the parachute at?" Adam asks, searching everywhere one might search for such a thing. "Well, there is no parachute," I say, becoming Mr. Rogers on a dime. "NO PARACHUTE?" Adam squeals, a bit worked up, "Well, what we sposed ta do if THIS SHIT CRASHES?" Now I'm Mr. Rogers on Valium. "Well, I'll tell you what to do in the event of a crash." They could not be one bit more attentive. "Are your seat belts securely fastened?" They check and nod earnestly. "Okay, now lean forward." They are very compliant. "No, you have to lean as far as you can—is that as far as you can go?" They are so low, I can barely register the nodding of their heads. "Okay," I say, steady and calm as she goes, "Now . . . if you can reach . . . kiss your asses good-bye . . . cuz that's all you'll be able to do if this thing goes down." They can't even believe that their chain has been yanked so egregiously. "*Qué gacho,* right there." "You . . . ain't . . . right."

Takeoff (as is always the case with novice homie flyers) transforms these two big gangsters into old ladies on a roller coaster. As usual, there is great sighing and clutching and rapid signs of the cross. Adam and Ricky can't take their eyes off the tiny window to their right and manage plenty of "Oh, my God's" and "This is proper." Terror melting into wonder, then slipping into peace. The peanuts and sodas are delivered, and they feel special (they later report to those back at the office, "They EVEN gave us peanuts!"). Then, after we climb above the bounce, Ricky pats Adam's chest, as they both look out above their own clouds, and whispers, "I love doing this with you, brother."

Life, after unspeakable loss, becoming poetry again. In this together, two brothers, locked arms, delighting in the view from up here.

Thomas Merton writes, "No despair of ours can alter the reality of things, or stain the joy of the cosmic dance which is always there . . . We are invited to forget ourselves on purpose, cast our awful solemnity to the winds and join in the general dance." The cosmic dance is simply always happening, and you'll want to be there when it happens. For it is there in the birth of your first child, in roundhouse bagging, in watching your crew eat, in an owl's surprising appearance, and in a "digested" frog. Rascally inventions of holiness abounding—today, awaiting the attention of our delight. Yes, yes, yes. God so loved the world that He thought we'd find the poetry in it. Music. Nothing playing.

8

Success

Peple want me to tell them success stories. I understand this. They are the stories you want to tell, after all. So why does my scalp tighten whenever I am asked this? Surely, part of it comes from my being utterly convinced I'm a fraud.

I find Bill Cain's reflection on the Shroud of Turin very consoling. He prefers frauds. He says, "If the shroud is a fraud then it is this masterful work of art. If it's the real thing, it's just dirty laundry."

Twenty years of this work has taught me that God has greater comfort with inverting categories than I do. What is success and what is failure? What is good and what is bad? Setback or progress? Great stock these days, especially in nonprofits (and who can blame them), is placed in evidence-based outcomes. People, funders in particular, want to know if what you do "works."

Are you, in the end, successful? Naturally, I find myself heartened by Mother Teresa's take: "We are not called to be successful, but faithful." This distinction is helpful for me as I barricade myself against the daily dread of setback. You need protection from the ebb and flow of three steps forward, five steps backward. You trip over disappointment and recalcitrance every day, and it all becomes a muddle. God intends it to be, I think. For once you choose to hang out with folks who carry more burden than they can bear, all bets seem to be off. Salivating for success keeps you from being faithful, keeps you from truly seeing whoever's sitting in front of you. Embracing a strategy and an approach you can believe in is sometimes the best you can do on any given day. If you surrender your need for results and outcomes, success becomes God's business. I find it hard enough to just be faithful.

In the first chapter, I mentioned Scrappy, whom I hired on our graffiti crew. He was the one, in a previous incarnation, who pulled a gun out on me and regretted the reputation he'd spent twenty years building. Just a few short months into his employment with us, he was gunned down at 5:30 in the morning while rolling a paintbrush over some graffiti in Boyle Heights. The detectives let me cross the police yellow tape and permitted me to bless Scrappy. "He must have been killed," the detective tells me as he lifts the tape and I climb under it, "by the gang whose graffiti he was covering up." I think, *not likely*, as I see his head and what appears to be something of a clean execution. No one really knows exactly why this happened to him, though it seemed clear that it had nothing to do with Homeboy Industries and the removal of graffiti. Something evidently caught up with Scrappy. Maybe his past, maybe his recent present. Perhaps the prospect of leading a life, devoid of "reputation," by the rules, and in the slow pace of the right thing, was more terrifying than exhilarating for Scrappy. Maybe he displeased someone along the way. Sometimes the only thing you know is what something isn't.

Quite apart from the tragic blow Scrappy's death was for all of us who loved him was the heartbreaking fact that he'd missed his chance to live in another way. Like a child thrilled but terrified by his first swim in the ocean, floating, carried, restful because he was moving in a completely different way, the new scene, its strangeness, its immensity had scared him back into the life he knew. Was he a success story? Does he now appear in some column of failure as we tally up outcomes? The tyranny of success often can't be bothered with complexity. The tote board matters little when held up alongside Scrappy's intricate, tragic struggle to figure out who he was in the world.

Two months later, another of our graffiti workers, Raul, was gunned down in one of our trucks, alone, parked/idling on First Street in front of the post office shortly after noon. Again, what one comes to know is what this death wasn't. Surely, it was not about Homeboy or connected in any way to graffiti or its removal. Equally certain is that it had no connection to Scrappy's death.

Just before Raul's death, I had walked the few short blocks from Homeboy to my Jesuit community for lunch, and as I'm returning, I see Hector, whom everyone calls Fro (for the enormous Afro he sported in those days) running toward me. My heart caves in as I see him, his hair lively, bouncing back and forth as he grows frantic to reach me. I go to the hospital, and Raul dies there, while his mother's screams pierce our hearts.

I used to tell homies that one of the reasons they continued to gangbang was they were never around to hear a mother scream when she heard her son was dead. I became something of a dreaded figure, I suppose—not unlike the uniformed officer knocking on the door of the family of the soldier serving in Iraq.

The mother pulls back the drape, looks out the window, and knows what news he's bringing. More times than I even want to recall, I've knocked on the door, anytime, day or middle of the night, when the mother sees me, I always just blurt it out: "*Lo mataron* a Richie." It seems kinder, in the end, not to cloud the moment with undue prelude. And the screaming is devastatingly painful to behold. More than anything I know. With Latinas, the screams become yelps, a primordial, indigenous sound. The mother's rocking back and forth, with continuous wailing, can be upsetting enough to alter behavior.

I remember once (and only once) seeing all the homies gathered together plotting vengeance, immediately after the shooting of their homie Victor. They were all "posted up" in front of his house in the projects, his mother sitting on the front steps, worried about Victor's condition. Then I arrive. I lean over and whisper to her (having just returned from the hospital) that Victor is dead. And this time the homies are there to hear. Instant wailing, syncopated yelps, screams that curdle your insides. The homies didn't do anything that night. They went home instead. The price of it all delivered to them, courtesy of a grieving mother's vocal chords.

After spending the entire afternoon with Raul's mom and family, I wanted to get back to the office before closing time. I knew that the homies needed to see me, and I, them. With ten minutes left on the day's clock, my workers filed into my tiny office, one by one, to hug, to cry some, and to take my emotional temperature. Each one attentive, tender, and consumed by a self-forgetfulness that only saints, really, are able to pull off.

Then I am there alone with the ache that doesn't leave you and the echoey silence of the vacated headquarters. Even the ghosts of the place seemed to have stepped out, when Freddy, one of my workers, appears, standing in my doorway. He asks how I'm doing, and I sigh, beckoning him to sit.

"I know your heart is breaking," he says, beginning to cry. "I wish I had a magic wand to pass over your pain." As an adult, I can't recall ever crying with another person more fully than at that moment. We both just lose ourselves in sobbing. Usually, I'd put myself, as the homies say, "on check status," but even I couldn't pull this off at the moment. I'd been holding this enormous, outsize grief "in check" for so long and had sudden permission to release it in the gentle urging and vast heart of Freddy. At twenty-three years old, he had worked at Homeboy for some years now in a wide variety of sites and tasks, but his singularly spectacular temper required frequent changes of venue. First the silkscreen plant, then the bulky-item drop-off center, and now, here at the headquarters. He surely, at this moment, knew how to use his deep rage and essential wound to hold all that I was carrying.

"You know, all of us here are drowning," Freddy begins with difficulty, the tears a tide that he's swimming against. "And YOU . . . you just reach in . . . and sweep us up." We resume our wailing, holding our heads, rocking some, unable to speak. Then Freddy, with his teeth clenched, and something nearly resembling his frequent bursts of anger, points his finger at me with a holy determination.

"I swear to you," he says, "If someone offered me a choice— right now—a million dollars or a chance to swoop ya up—" Freddie stops and swallows hard against this overflow of crying. "I . . . would . . . swoop . . . you . . . up." Through my tears, I am barely able to eke out, "You just did . . . you just did."

Sr. Elaine Roulette, the founder of My Mother's House in New York, was asked, "How do you work with the poor?" She answered, "You don't. You share your life with the poor." It's as basic as crying together. It is about "casting your lot" before it ever becomes about "changing their lot."

Success and failure, ultimately, have little to do with living the gospel. Jesus just stood with the outcasts until they were welcomed or until he was crucified—whichever came first.

The American poet Jack Gilbert writes, "The pregnant heart is driven to hopes that are the wrong size for this world." The strategy and stance of Jesus was consistent in that it was always out of step with the world. Jesus defied all the categories upon which the world insisted: good-evil, success-failure, pure-impure. Surely, He was an equal-opportunity "pisser off-er" in this regard. The right wing would stare at Him and question where He chose to stand. They hated that He aligned Himself with the unclean, those outside—those folks you ought neither to touch nor be near. He hobnobbed with the leper, shared table fellowship with the sinner, and rendered Himself ritually impure in the process. They found it offensive that, to boot, Jesus had no regard for their wedge issues, their constitutional amendments or their culture wars.

The Left was equally annoyed. They wanted to see the ten-point plan, the revolution in high gear, the toppling of sinful social structures. They were impatient with His brand of solidarity. They wanted to see Him taking the right stand on issues, not just standing in the right place.

But Jesus just stood with the outcast. The Left screamed: "Don't just stand there, do something." And the Right maintained: "Don't stand with those folks at all." Both sides, seeing

Jesus as the wrong size for this world, came to their own reasons for wanting Him dead. Both sides were equally impressed as He unrolled the scroll and spoke of "good news to the poor" . . . "sight to the blind" . . . "liberty to captives." Yet only a handful of verses later, they want to throw Jesus over a cliff.

How do we get the world to change anyway? Dorothy Day asked critically: "Where were the saints to try and change the social order? Not just minister to the slaves, but to do away with slavery." Dorothy Day is a hero of mine, but I disagree with her here. You actually abolish slavery by accompanying the slave. We don't strategize our way out of slavery, we solidarize, if you will, our way toward its demise. We stand in solidarity with the slave, and by so doing, we diminish slavery's ability to stand. By casting our lot with the gang member, we hasten the demise of demonizing. All Jesus asks is, *"Where are you standing?"* And after chilling defeat and soul-numbing failure, He asks again, "Are you still standing there?"

Can we stay faithful and persistent in our fidelity even when things seem not to succeed? I suppose Jesus could have chosen a strategy that worked better (evidenced-based outcomes)—that didn't end in the Cross—but he couldn't find a strategy more soaked with fidelity than the one he embraced.

* * *

I am in a rush one late afternoon and driving out of the church parking lot, when La Shady stands right in front of my car. She's a big girl of nineteen, large hipped and breasted, looking more like a woman of twice her age. Cradled in her right arm and resting on her sizable right hip is her one-year-old daughter, Jennifer.

Shady's "man" and father of her daughter was Leonardo, whom I had buried three months before. In a fracas in the gas station at Fourth and Boyle, between Leonardo and five members of a rival gang, a nervous, tiny gang member, viewing the fight from inside the car, fumbled with a gun and shot wildly at those duking it out. His bullet found Leonardo.

Shady uses the hand not attached to her daughter to serve as a stop sign in front of my car, and she rushes over to my open window on the driver's side. She leans in and kisses me. She's draped in a huge black-and-white Raiders jersey with a number on the front.

"Where ya goin', G?"

I know enough not to tell her. I'm heading to a peace-treaty meeting I've set up between the female members of her gang and the one that killed her man. She would have been one I'd consider too much of a hothead, and even so, the rawness of Leonardo's death is still too dominant in the ring for her, knocking out reason, calm, and any hope for peace. She is not on my invitation list.

"I'm going on an errand."

Girls in gangs really represent just a tiny percentage of the overall gang population. The numbers vary from 5 to 10 percent. I would suggest favoring the lower number. Gangs are a guy thing, primarily. It is far more common to have gang molls—the girls who dated the guys in one gang as opposed to those in another. Those who are actually "jumped in" to neighborhoods perform reconnaissance, stir things up, and often shame the males into fighting—"Are you going to let that *vato* just walk over there, across the street and NOT do anything about it?"

The only times I've ever been remotely hurt in all these years always came in breaking up fights between girl gang members. Guys would stop the second I'd arrive. The parting of the Red Sea of brawling homies as I'd make my way through them. Girls, on the other hand, require back up. You can't get them to stop. ALWAYS bring someone with you to break things up.

Shady is a tough one. There is a certain gruffness to her, and when she's not of a hard-edged mind, she's impossibly shy. This seems to be that rare moment in which she is neither rough nor retiring. She is atypically glad to see me and has an urgency to talk I don't recognize.

"G, you got two minutes? I had a dream last night, and I need you to explain it to me." (Homies always thought I possessed the lexicon to dream interpretation. I did nothing to encourage this. They just presumed it was part of my credentials.) She crouches closer to me and gives Jennifer a good hop to readjust her on her hip. She leans left to accommodate her there.

In the dream she enters Dolores Mission Church at night, and as she walks down the center aisle, she sees, in this dimly lit place, me standing up in front, vested for Mass. By my side is the coffin of a tiny baby, and the lid is up. Shady doesn't walk closer at first, but I summon and wave her forward. She trusts me enough to keep walking, but she admits she is absolutely terrified to peer into this coffin. I'm smiling and encouraging her to keep going. Shady finally reaches the casket and dares to peek. But before Shady can even fully get her head over the tiny box, a white dove flies out of it, startling her. It circles the inside of the church and flies above, back and forth, until it lands on her shoulder. Then she wakes up.

"What's it mean, G?"

"Well, it's obvious what it means," I say, clueless as to the dream's meaning. Since I was late for a summit and because my sense of Shady's mood, generally, is that she is one to dig in the heels of her Nike Cortez and not "give peace a chance," I self-servingly give her my take.

"Well, everyone knows that the white dove stands for peace. And so God is asking you to move toward forgiveness and healing and peace. And everything's gonna be fine."

She listens, but there are wheels turning that seem to be operating well out of my view. I abandon my own tight grasp on punctuality, and for the first time I really see her standing in front of me, juggling her daughter, her Raiders jersey flapping with the wind. I place my hand on her forearm, resting on the door of my car.

"But here's the only thing that matters, kiddo. How did the dream make you feel?" Shady begins to cry, and her daughter, curious at first, soon joins Shady in sympathy.

"That's the thing, G. At first I was scared, like . . . maybe that's my daughter in the casket. But when I saw the bird, I only felt peace and love in my heart."

I had not ever seen Shady cry like this.

"God only wants you to feel those things, *mijita*—love in your heart . . . peace. You're okay."

She reached into the car with more verve than usual, nearly whomping Jennifer in the head, as she threw her arms around me, squeezing hard and thanking me harder.

At close to midnight that same day, Shady is crammed into the middle seat in the back of a car filled with gang members. They've driven well out of her barrio, and the guys in the car are from a neighborhood not her own. They drive, and hand signs get thrown out the window at rivals standing on some street corner. The corner guys yell and scream all manner of foulness at the car, and Shady and the gang squeal rubber out of there, laughing. Not a block away, a corner *vato* finds his gun. Shady slumps in the backseat. Only one bullet entered the car that night, and it happened to find the back of Shady's head.

Now what does the dream mean, told to me just hours before Shady's life was to end? I have no idea. Except that we are unfailingly called to stand with Shady and all those who grieved her passing. Beyond that, I don't really know. Allowing our hearts to "be broken by the very thing that breaks the heart of God." In the end, what needs to get disrupted will find its disruption in our solidarity and in our intimate kinship with the outcast—who too infrequently knows the peace of a white dove resting on a shoulder. What is the failure of death, after all, when it is measured against what rises in you when you catch sight of this white bird?

Nietzsche writes, "The weight of all things needs to be measured anew." Enough death and tragedy come your way, and who would blame you for wanting a new way to measure.

If we choose to stand in the right place, God, through us, creates a community of resistance without our even realizing it. To embrace the strategy of Jesus is to be engaged in what Dean Brackley calls "downward mobility." Our locating ourselves with those who have been endlessly excluded becomes an act of visible protest. For no amount of our screaming at the people in charge to change things can change them. The margins don't get erased by simply insisting that the powers-that-be erase them. The trickle-down theory doesn't really work here. The powers bent on waging war against the poor and the young and the "other" will only be moved to kinship when they observe it. Only when we can see a community where the outcast is valued and appreciated will we abandon the values that seek to exclude.

Jesus was always too busy being faithful to worry about success. I'm not opposed to success; I just think we should accept it only if it is a by-product of our fidelity. If our primary concern is results, we will choose to work only with those who give us good ones.

Myriad are the examples at Homeboy Industries of homies coloring way outside the lines and being given their ninety-eighth chance. Maybe it's because we are often forced to start where others have stopped. Some on my senior staff wanted to change our motto, printed on our T-shirts, from "Nothing stops a bullet like a job" to "You just can't disappoint us enough." Others would mention that there seem to be no consequences for some actions, and, of course, in the real world, there are consequences. Someone told me once, "I mean, what's it take to get fired at Homeboy—release nerve gas?" When it seems the best thing for a person, I have, often enough, fired someone. I call the person in and say, "The day won't ever come when I will withdraw love and support from you. I am simply in your corner till the wheels fall off. Oh, by the way, I have to let you go." They always agree with me. Nearly always.

There is no question that everybody working at Homeboy would have been fired anyplace else (including me, I suppose—just ask my board). But as Mark Torres, S.J., beloved spiritual guide at Homeboy Industries, says, "We see in the homies what they don't see in themselves, until they do."

There was a homegirl, straight out of prison, with award-winning and alarming tattoos all over her face. She began work at the silkscreen. First day, a fight. Second day, she came utterly illuminated on "chronic" (marijuana). Third day, she arrived at work, in a car filled with her homies (this is against our rules). Oh, and the car was stolen (this is against, well, everybody's rules). I suppose we could have fired her. And yet we decided, with all the "no matter whatness" we could muster, that she would give up on us long before we would ever give up on her. And give up she did. She just stopped showing up. We'll be ready for her when she comes back. You stand with the least likely to succeed until success is succeeded by something more valuable: kinship. You stand with the belligerent, the surly, and the badly behaved until bad behavior is recognized for the language it is: the vocabulary of the deeply wounded and of those whose burdens are more than they can bear.

Jesus jostled irreparably the purity code of the shot callers of His day. He recognized that it was precisely this code that kept folks from kinship. Maybe success has become the new purity code. And Jesus shows us that the desire for purity (nine times out of ten) is, in fact, the enemy of the gospel.

Funders sometimes say, "We don't fund efforts; we fund outcomes." We all hear this and think how sensible, practical, realistic, hard-nosed, and clear-eyed it is. But maybe Jesus doesn't know why we're nodding so vigorously. Without wanting to, we sometimes allow our preference for the poor to morph into a preference for the well-behaved and the most likely to succeed, *even* if you get better outcomes when you work with those folks. If success is our engine, we sidestep the difficult and belligerent and eventually abandon "the slow work of God."

Failure and death become insurmountable.

*   *   *

I see Manny in the neighborhood, and I am not one bit happy. Once homies move away from the projects, I tell them they have no more business here.

Once I saw a homie named Mugsy, now in his early thirties, three kids, lives away from the neighborhood, good construction job, *and* he's in the barrio.

"So what the hell are you doin' here?" I ask him.

"Oh, just going to buy some beer at Moon's store."

"Look, dog, you can buy beer anywhere."

"Yeah, but," he says, "not every place accepts food stamps." The fact that I rarely win these battles does not keep me from the "broken record" of my insisting.

When I see Manny, I begin calmly, "Okay, Manny, what are you doing here?" Manny wants to defuse quickly, "Oh, I'm just visiting."

I turn my voice into a hospital's loudspeaker: "MAY I HAVE YOUR ATTENTION PLEASE. VISITING HOURS ARE NOW OVER."

Manny knows enough to change the subject. "Go ahead and congratulate me," he says.

"For what?" I concede, air hissing out of my balloon.

"On Monday, I begin college—at Rio Hondo."

"Son, I'm proud of you—now go home."

Manny had been one of twenty workers from a variety of gangs who built our child care center. It took them two years to build. It would have taken professional types four months, tops. We opted, instead, to begin the "Wrong Size for This World" construction crew. Nothing made Manny prouder than to have his name inscribed on the building's wall. "I built that," he'd say.

Not three hours later, as Manny pulls onto the ramp for the

freeway home, a rival sees him and opens up fire. Within hours, the doctors are enlisting me to convince the family to donate Manny's organs.

These things take time. For several days, I join in the vigil with his lady Irma, eight months pregnant with their second child. She does not leave his side. I stop asking her to take periodic respites. She lines the bed tray with photos, mutually meaningful, of Manny Jr. and the family altogether.

I watch as an endless procession of homies and family members and friends come through to say good-bye to Manny's comatose body. The homies tenderly drape rosarios around his neck and kiss him and hug him. Across Manny's chest is a tattoo of the song title "I'm Still Here," which he put on the last time he was shot.

Standing in the room, I return to some months before when Manny had called me, quite *panickeado* about something—usually he called about his fear of violating probation again. I meet him at the iron stairwell outside of Irma's apartment in the projects. When I get there, he is already crying. It occurs to me to ask him, well into our conversation, "What do you want, Manny?" He knows what I'm talking about.

What do you most deeply, truly want?

Manny closes his eyes and folds his hands, and the obvious intensity may well burst something. He has the look of a man who, if he can articulate this correctly, might set himself on the right path. When Manny returns from his search, he says only, "I just want to be a good father. But I don't know how to be one." Guideposts were not plentiful. I had buried his own father of a heroin overdose the year before, and his childhood was surrounded by good people intractably stuck in the chaos that only

PCP can produce. When I met him years and years before, he was a little kid whose room and sanctuary was a closet.

I finally get Manny's grandmother to sign the release to donate his organs. "Not his eyes, though," she says, "Not his eyes."

As the two nurses wheel Manny to surgery for the harvesting of his organs, one nurse turns to the other and shakes her head in disgust, no doubt eyeing Manny's tattoos.

"I mean," she says, rolling her eyes, "who would want this monster's heart?" The other nurse stops the gurney midhallway and turns on her coworker with a clarity that may well have surprised herself. "How dare you call this kid a monster? Didn't you see his family, his friends, his son? He was nineteen years old, for God's sakes. He belonged to somebody. Shame on you." I only know this happened because I gave an in-service to the nurses at White Memorial Hospital. The chastising nurse tearfully told her story, in front of everybody, during the Q and A.

"I cried all the way home that night," she said.

Obviously, after having buried 168 young human beings, all killed violently because of gangs, I have had to come to terms with the "failure" of death.

"Death, where is your sting?"

La muerte, ya no tiene dominio are words I've spoken from the pulpit many times. Death has no power. Easy for me to say. There is much self-protection in saying it, however, otherwise you fear actually losing your mind. Annie Dillard writes, "So once in Israel, love came to us incarnate and stood in the doorway between two worlds, and we were all afraid." Working with gang members means always trying to make sense of life in the doorway. Yes, the wheat dies, but check out the fruit. Sure there is pain in childbirth, but here's this kid. Who's still looking at the ashes, once the phoenix has risen? You're always on the lookout for fates worse than death, and it turns out, there are a slew of them.

An Algerian monk, threatened with death, says to those who will inflict it: "What do we have to fear after all? To be thrown into the tenderness of God?" That's certainly where I want to be, even if on most days the fear seems to triumph.

The owner of a vast, expansive heart and among the most heroic women I know is Soledad, the mother of four. I met her second oldest, Ronnie, when he was a sophomore at Roosevelt High School. I suspect he began working at our office, after school, shortly after his brother Angel started to work at our silk-screen factory. Angel was from a gang and two years older than Ronnie, who was never from any barrio.

Shortly after 9/11, Ronnie got his diploma (didn't even graduate on stage) and joined the marines. Once, he and Soledad visited me so I could give a special blessing for Ronnie, who was headed to some secret location (which turned out to be Afghanistan). Sometime later, Ronnie was home on leave and walking back to the house after a midnight run to Jack in the Box.

Soledad can hear from the bedroom the most dreaded question in the barrio: someone is "hitting up" Ronnie. "Where you from?"

If you are not from a gang, you say, "I ain't from nowhere." Variations on this can be, "I don't bang." This could mean, "I am a gang member, but I don't play that anymore," or "I am not a gang member."

She strains to hear what he says. He might have laughed or even said, "the marines." She needs no straining to hear the shots that follow. Ronnie dies in her arms outside their kitchen door. He is shot four times in the back and twice in the head. They shot his hand off. Ronnie was given a full military burial. Soledad was handed a folded flag.

For the next six months, there was no consoling Soledad. She quit her job and rarely left the house. She dressed in black every day, bathed infrequently, didn't bother with hair or makeup.

Among my proudest possessions is a photograph of Angel, her oldest son, in burgundy gown and gold sash and mortar board at his graduation from Roosevelt. Very few homies pull this off, and Angel was deservedly proud.

Angel sits his mother down on a Sunday morning, six months after Ronnie's death.

"Look," he says to Soledad, "you have to stop this. You have three kids left, and we need you. So I want you to go throw these black clothes away, take a bath, do your hair, and put some makeup on. It's time."

Soledad's firstborn breaks through the solid mass of grief that had encased her soul and left her heart immobile for all this time. So she does it. Bathes, wears something with color in it, fixes her hair, and puts on makeup. She emerges from her room, and she is radiant. Angel cups her face in his hands, "You look gorgeous." He doesn't hesitate to add, "It's about damn time."

That afternoon, Angel is sitting on his front porch, eating a sandwich, and there is a commotion down the block. There is a kid running with all his might. He is from Angel's barrio. He is being chased by two enemies. When they catch up to him, the kid is able to disappear from their sight. This leaves the two panting in front of Angel's front porch. He knows enough to scramble wildly toward his front door. The shooting begins, and

Soledad runs to the source of the sound. She would say later that she wished the shooters hadn't left until they had also killed her.

It being Sunday, I was celebrating Mass in the varied detention facilities, so I came late to the news of Angel's death. By the time I reach Soledad's living room later that day, she is huddled in a corner. Forget Kleenex. Forget handkerchief. Soledad is sobbing into a huge bath towel. And the few of us there found our arms too short to wrap around this kind of pain.

I see Soledad a lot, but this one day, two years after the death of Angel, I see her in front of the office and we hug.

"How ya doin, kiddo?"

Soledad grabs my arm and thinks and considers her words.

"You know, I love the two kids that I have. I hurt for the two that are gone." She begins to cry and shows the slightest embarrassment at the size of her honesty.

"The hurt wins . . . the hurt wins."

Two months later, Soledad is taken to the hospital for an irregular heartbeat and chest pain. I visit her in her room, and she tells me what happened the night she came to the emergency room. They have her on a gurney in White Memorial's ER. The doctors are tending to her with EKGs and the like, when there is a rush of activity at the entrance. With a flurry of bodies and medical staff moving into their proscribed roles, a teenage gang member is rushed to the vacant space right next to Soledad. The kid is covered in blood from multiple gunshot wounds, and they begin cutting off his clothes. The wounds are too serious to waste time pulling the curtain that separates Soledad from this kid fighting for his life. People are pounding on his chest and inserting IVs. Soledad turns and sees him. She recognizes him as a kid from the gang that most certainly robbed her of her sons.

"As I saw this kid," she tells me, "I just kept thinking of what my friends might say if they were here with me. They'd say, 'Pray that he dies.'" But she just looked at this tiny kid, struggling to sidestep the fate of her sons, as the doctors work and scream, "WE'RE LOSING HIM. WE'RE LOSING HIM."

"And I began to cry as I have never cried before and started to pray the hardest I've ever prayed. 'Please . . . don't . . . let him die. I don't want his mom to go through what I have.'"

And the kid lived. Sometimes, it only seems that the hurt wins.

Mary Oliver writes, "There are things you can't reach. But you can reach out to them, and all day long."

In the end, effective outcomes and a piling of success stories aren't the things for which we reach. Though, who am I kidding, I prefer them to abject failure and decades of death. But it's not about preference. It's about the disruption of categories that leads us to abandon the difficult, the disagreeable, and the least likely to go very far. On most days, if I'm true to myself, I just want to share my life with the poor, regardless of result. I want to lean into the challenge of intractable problems with as tender a heart as I can locate, knowing that there is some divine ingenuity here, "the slow work of God," that gets done if we're faithful. Maybe the world could use a dose of a wrong-size approach; otherwise the hurt wins. Maybe there are things you can't reach. But you can stretch your arm across a gurney and forgive and heal.

Equal souls. All day long.

9

Kinship

Mother Teresa diagnosed the world's ills in this way: we've just "forgotten that we belong to each other." Kinship is what happens to us when we refuse to let that happen. With kinship as the goal, other essential things fall into place; without it, no justice, no peace. I suspect that were kinship our goal, we would no longer be promoting justice—we would be celebrating it.

Kinship has a way of sneaking up on you even as you seek to create it. I celebrate Catholic services, on a rotating basis, in twenty-five detention institutions in Los Angeles County—juvenile halls, probation camps, jails, and state youth authority facilities. After Mass, in the gym or chapel or classroom, I hand out my card. The infomercial is always the same:

"Call me when you get out. I'll hook you up with a job— take off your tattoos—line ya up with a counselor. I won't know where you are, but with this card, you'll know where I am. Don't slow drag. Cuz if you do, you'll get popped again and end up right back here. So call me."

I hand out thousands of cards a year.

So a homie named Louie, seventeen years old, appears in my office one day, bright, happy, and smiling. Never in my life had I seen more hickeys on a human being than on this guy. His entire neck is spotted with these *chupetonazos*. Even his cheeks are covered. I'm thinking Mr. Guinness of the world records might be interested in talking to Louie.

"So, here I am," he says, arms outstretched, "I just got out yesterday," and he points at me with glee, "and YOU . . . are the VERY FIRST person I came to see."

I look at this giddy gang member and say, "Louie . . . I have a feeling I was your second stop."

The two of us collapse in laughter and, suddenly, there's kinship so quickly. Not service provider and service recipient. No daylight to separate—just "us."

Exactly what God had in mind.

Often we strike the high moral distance that separates "us" from "them," and yet it is God's dream come true when we recognize that there exists no daylight between us. Serving others is good. It's a start. But it's just the hallway that leads to the Grand Ballroom.

Kinship—not serving the other, but being one with the other. Jesus was not "a man for others"; he was one with them. There is a world of difference in that.

* * *

I suppose I never felt this kinship more keenly in my own life than when I was first diagnosed with leukemia. At this writing, I am several years cancer free. Not long ago, a homie breathlessly said to me, "I hear your cancer's in intermission." My leukemia has been in the lobby ever since, waiting in line for popcorn.

The news of my illness first managed to reach most folks by way of the front page of the Sunday *Los Angeles Times*. Word spread—homies came out of the woodwork. My voicemail began to fill.

"Now it's our turn to take care of you," says Lala, a homegirl I've known forever.

A huge homie named Fernie stands in front of my desk, tattooed and something of a fullback to whom God had forgotten to give a neck. Tears glistening in his eyes.

"What do I have that you need?" he says. Meaning organs.

I was more than a little happy to tell him that I wasn't in need of any.

At some point in midchemotherapy, I arrive at my office after a treatment. A tiny, fifteen-year-old gang member plunks himself down in the chair facing my desk. He looks positively stricken.

"I hear you have leukemia," his voice cracks.

I nod solemnly.

There is an awkward silence, which he finally fills.

"My cat had leukemia."

This just sits in the air.

"Yeah," he says. "She died."

"Oh," I say, "really sorry to hear that . . . Awfully glad ya stopped by, though . . . you really, uh . . . picked me up, right there." My favorite moment of all, though, came when P-Nut called me from jail. Collect. He had just read the news in the paper.

"Hey," he says, screaming over the jailhouse din. "What's with this leukemia anyway?"

"Well, it's cancer . . . in the blood. The doctor says my white count is too high."

P-Nut is immediately dismissive.

"Damn . . . these doctors," I can hear him shaking his head. "They don't be knowin' nuthin'."

"Whadda ya mean?"

"I mean, HEEEELLLLOOOO!!! 'Course your white count's high . . . YOU WHITE!!!"

I'm accepting more collect calls from jail now and calling them "second opinions."

* * *

No daylight to separate us.

Only kinship. Inching ourselves closer to creating a community of kinship such that God might recognize it. Soon we imagine, with God, this circle of compassion. Then we imagine no one standing outside of that circle, moving ourselves closer to the margins so that the margins themselves will be erased. We stand there with those whose dignity has been denied. We locate ourselves with the poor and the powerless and the voiceless. At the edges, we join the easily despised and the readily left out. We stand with the demonized so that the demonizing will stop. We situate ourselves right next to the disposable so that the day will come when we stop throwing people away. The prophet Habakkuk writes, "The vision still has its time, presses on to fulfillment and it will not disappoint . . . and if it delays, wait for it."

Kinship is what God presses us on to, always hopeful that its time has come.

*   *   *

I don't recognize Lencho when he steps into my office. Though that is the first question he asked. "'Member me?" Truth is, I don't. He is two days fresh out of Corcoran State Prison. He has been locked up for ten years—a juvenile tried as an adult. He was fourteen years old when I met him at Central Juvenile Hall. Now at twenty-four, his arms are all "sleaved out"—every inch covered in tattoos. His neck is blackened by the name of his gang—stretching from jawbone to collarbone. His head is shaved and covered with alarming tattoos. Most startling of all (though impressive) are two exquisitely etched devil's horns planted on his forehead.

He says, "You know . . . I'm having a hard time finding a job."

I think, *Well, maybe we can put our heads together on this one.*

I'm about to nudge him in the direction of our tattoo-removal clinic, when he says, "I've never had a job in my life—been locked up since I was a kid."

I suggest that we change this. I tell him to begin work tomorrow, Tuesday, at Homeboy Silkscreen. In operation for more than ten years, nearly five hundred rival gang members have worked there, screen printing and embroidering apparel for more than 2,500 customers. On Wednesday, I call the Homeboy Silkscreen factory to check on *Chamuco* (the affectionate way of addressing Satan), our newest worker. Lencho is brought to the phone.

"So," I ask, "How's it feel to be a workin' man?"

"It feels proper," he says, "In fact, I'm like that *vato* in the commercial—you know the guy—the one who keeps walkin' up to total strangers and says, 'I just lowered my cholesterol.' Yeah. That's me right there."

I admit to him that this whole cholesterol thing has flown right over my head.

"I mean, yesterday, after work, I'm sittin' at the back a' the bus, dirty and tired, and, I mean, I just couldn't help myself. I kept turning to total strangers—'Just comin' back, first day on the job.' (He turns to another.) 'Just gettin' off—my first day at work.'"

He tells me this, and I can't help but imagine the people on the bus—half wondering if mothers are clutching their kids more closely. Surely someone is overhearing Lencho and thinking: *"Bien hecho—nice goin'."* I suspect it's equally certain that someone catching Lencho's outburst reflects inwardly, *What a waste of a perfectly good job.*

The wrong idea has taken root in the world. And the idea is this: there just might be lives out there that matter less than other lives. The prophet Jeremiah writes: "In this place of which you say it is a waste . . . there will be heard again the voice of mirth and the voice of gladness . . . the voices of those who sing."

Lencho's voice matters. To that end, we choose to become what child psychiatrist Alice Miller calls "enlightened witnesses"—people who through their kindness, tenderness, and focused, attentive love return folks to themselves. It is a returning—not a measuring up. Lencho is returned to himself and announces this with clarion voice at the back of a bus. We don't hold the bar up and ask people to measure up to it. One simply shows up and commits to telling the truth.

At Homeboy Industries, we seek to tell each person this truth: they are exactly what God had in mind when God made them—and then we watch, from this privileged place, as people inhabit this truth. Nothing is the same again. No bullet can pierce this, no prison walls can keep this out. And death can't touch it—it is just that huge.

But much stands in the way of this liberating truth. You need to dismantle shame and disgrace, coaxing out the truth in people who've grown comfortable believing its opposite.

One day, I have three homies in my car as I am headed to give a talk. While there, they will set up a table and sell Homeboy/Homegirl merchandise. Our banter in the car spans the range of bagging on each other. We laugh a lot, and I am distracted enough not to notice that the gas tank is on empty. I lean into JoJo, the homie occupying shotgun.

"*Oye*, dog, be on the lookout for a gas station."

He doesn't seem to wholly trust my judgment. He leans toward the gas gauge and dismisses my call.

"You're fine," he says.

"*Cómo que* I'm fine—I'm on *ÉCHALE, cabrón*." Waving at him, I say, "HELLO, E means empty."

JoJo looks at me with bonafide shock.

"E means empty?"

"Well, yeah, what did ya think it meant?"

"Enough."

"Well, what did ya think F stood for?"

"Finished."

After I thank him for visiting our planet—I realize that this is exactly how the dismantling process has to play itself out. Homies stare into the mirror and pronounce "EMPTY." Our collective task is to suggest instead "ENOUGH"—enough gifts, enough talent, enough goodness. When you have enough, there's plenty.

Or if their verdict is "FINISHED," we are asked to lead them instead to "fullness"—the place within—where they find in themselves exactly what God had in mind. It would be hard to overstate how daunting it is to conjure new images and reconstruct messages.

* * *

When Richard arrived at Homeboy Industries, he was a nineteen-year-old for whom sadness was a constant refrain. Smiles were occasional and fleeting. He would tend toward beating himself up—often for being the only gang member in his family. He said to me once, "I'm the black sheep in my family" (farm animals not his strong suit). After meeting my older brother and his wife, he asked plaintively, "What's your brother do for a living?"

"Well, he's a principal—at an elementary school in San Diego."

"And your *cuñada*?"

"She's a nurse at an intensive care unit in a hospital."

"Damn, G," he says, shaking his head with gravity and sadness, "everyone in your family IS somebody." Which I suppose meant that no one in Richard's family was anyone and neither was he.

One day "out of the wild, blue yonder" (as the homies would say), Richard brings up the "flicka."

"Hey, G, I found this flicka [a photograph] of me yesterday," he said, speaking with more *animo* (enthusiasm) than I've ever seen.

"Yeah, it's a little tiny black-and-white flicka. Maybe I'm ten years old or something."

There seems to be no story to the photograph beyond just finding it. Days later, he returns to the subject, adding little.

"Yeah, I'm trippin' out on that flicka I found—it's a trip to see myself," he says.

"Yeah," I say, "you mentioned that the other day" (thinking, *and your point would be . . . ?*).

A week later, Richard appears in my office, smiling and seated in front of my desk. He wordlessly produces the photograph and hands it to me. It is no more than an inch square and reveals an unsmiling Richard at ten. He has a great shock of hair, and since, presently, Richard's head is shaved, it seems to be a conversation starter.

"You got hair, Richard," I say.

He just sits there. So I stare at the kid in the flicka and wonder if he is giving it to me. The only way to find out is to offer it back to him. I do, and he doesn't reach for it.

"D'ya think there is any way to make it big?"

"Sure, 'course we can," I say.

That week, I head to the Camera Store at the Montebello Town Center.

"May I help you, sir?" the guy asks.

"Yeah," I say, showing him the flicka, "Make it big."

The guy was having his doubts about being able to enlarge it much.

"Sir," I say, "you have to make this photograph larger than it is."

He worked his magic as best he could, and the picture grew to a nearly 4 × 4 inch photo, gaining a certain grainy, greenish hue in the process.

Richard beamed as he held the enlarged, framed, finished product.

This is not a story about a photograph. It is a story of the self made to feel too small from being bombarded with messages of shame and disgrace. People call you "the black sheep" long enough, you tend to believe them. So, we reach in, dismantle the message, and rearrange the language so you can imagine yourself as somebody.

I grew up in an old, large house. My five sisters and two brothers and I were told never to go to the attic. This is all we needed to hear. Before long, we were selling tickets to the attic. On one of our forays there, navigating the uncertain planks that kept you from falling through the ceiling below (I guess this explains my mom's prohibition), we found a box of old record albums. One thick, red-clay recording was labeled "O Holy Night"—Kathleen Conway (Conway was my mom's maiden name). We hurried downstairs, placed the record on our toy phonograph, and encircled the speakers, lying on our stomachs, fists propping up our attentive heads. A glorious, though timeworn and scratchy, voice came through the speakers. Our mom, it turns out, before she decided to have eight kids, was an opera singer. We could barely fathom that the voice that hollered at us to come to dinner belonged to this magic emerging from our toy phonograph. We played the grooves off of this record. Consequently, a line from the song found itself permanently etched in my brain—a mantra of sorts: "Long lay the world in sin and error pining—'til He appeared and the soul felt its worth." Sure—it's a song about Jesus and Christmas, but how is it not the job description of human beings seeking kinship. It's about "appearing," remembering that we belong to one another, and letting souls feel their worth.

* * *

Fifteen years ago, Bandit came to see me. He had been well named by his homies, being at home in all things illegal. He was "down for his varrio" and put in time running up to cars and selling crack in Aliso Village. He spent a lot of time locked up and had always seemed impervious to help. But then that day, fifteen years ago, his resistance broke. He sat in my office and said he was "tired of being tired." I escorted him to one of our four job developers and, as luck would have it, they located an entry-level job in a warehouse. Unskilled, low-paying, a first job.

Cut to fifteen years later, Bandit calls me near closing time on Friday. He now runs the warehouse, owns his own home, is married with three kids. I hadn't heard from him in some time. No news is usually good news with homies. He speaks in something like a breathless panic.

"G, ya gotta bless my daughter."

"Is she okay?" I ask. "I mean, is she sick—or in the hospital?"

"No, no," he says, "on Sunday, she's goin' to Humboldt College. Imagine, my oldest, my Carolina, goin' to college. But she's a little *chaparrita,* and I'm scared for her. So do ya think you could give her a little send-off *bendición?*

I schedule them to come the next day to Dolores Mission, where I have baptisms at one o'clock. Bandit, his wife, and three kids, including the college-bound Carolina, arrive at 12:30. I situate them all in front of the altar, Carolina planted in the middle. We encircle her, and I guide them to place their hands on her head or shoulder, to touch her as we close our eyes and bow our heads. Then, as the homies would say, I do a "long-ass prayer," and before we know it, we all become *chillones,* sniffling our way through this thing.

I'm not entirely sure why we're all crying, except, I suppose, for the fact that Bandit and his wife don't know anybody who's gone to college—except, I guess, me. Certainly no one in either one of their families. So we end the prayer, and we laugh at how mushy we all just got. Wiping our tears, I turn to Carolina and ask, "So, what are ya gonna study at Humboldt?"

She says without missing a beat,

"Forensic psychology."

"Daaamn, forensic psychology?"

Bandit chimes in, "Yeah, she wants to study the criminal mind."

Silence.

Carolina turns slowly to Bandit, holds up one hand, and points to her dad, her pointing finger blocked by her other hand, so he won't notice. We all notice and howl and Bandit says, "Yeah, I'm gonna be her first subject!"

We laugh and walk to the car. Everyone piles in, but Bandit hangs back. "Can I tell you something, dog?" I ask, standing in the parking lot. "I give you credit for the man you've chosen to become. I'm proud of you."

"*Sabes qué?*" he says, eyes watering, "I'm proud of myself. All my life, people called me a lowlife, a *bueno para nada*. I guess I showed 'em."

I guess he did.

And the soul feels its worth.

* * *

In the spring of 2005, First Lady Laura Bush chose Homeboy Industries as the only gang intervention program in the country to visit during her Helping America's Youth campaign. Since she couldn't visit all our sites, we decided that the locus of her visit would be the Homeboy Silkscreen factory. We and her people planned a mere one-hour stopover, which included a tour of homies screening shirts and a roundtable discussion with various participants and trainees from every corner of our organization. The visit went well, and the thirty-plus homies and homegirls invited to participate were all genuinely thrilled to be in the proximity of the wife of the president of the United States.

Al Gore had visited the Homeboy Bakery as vice president back in 1997. His arrival and that of Mrs. Bush brought teams of Secret Service agents to our place. Sharpshooters were placed on the roofs. Bomb-sniffing dogs were let loose, and severe, humorless agents asked me for the names, birthdates, and social security numbers of anyone within spittin' range of the vice president or Mrs. Bush. In both cases, after I had supplied a complete list, an agent returns to me, hems and haws with discomfort, and says, "Uh well, Father . . . I mean . . . these people HAVE RECORDS."

During the summer, after the First Lady's visit, I receive a call from a staffer for the First Lady, inviting me to speak at the Helping America's Youth conference at Howard University in DC in October. I accept, and she quickly adds that Mrs. Bush hopes I will bring "three homies" with me.

Now, whether the First Lady actually used the H word, I can't be certain. This woman informs me that after the all-day conference some of the participants will be invited to dinner at the White House. Certainly, crooks have resided at this house before, but it might well be the first time gang members have ever stepped foot inside the place.

I pick Alex, Charlie, and Felipe. I suppose if you had asked central casting to select three homies—they might have chosen these guys. All three are large, tattooed, had done time. They had the appearance of menace. Felipe had worked for me on the graffiti crew, right out of prison, before we got him a better job. He was a solid character, articulate and smart. I asked him to speak at the conference. Charlie, I had known for more than twenty years. He and his identical twin were fixtures in the projects—more enamored of smoking "kools" than gangbanging. Charlie has a prosthetic leg—his real leg was shot off by rivals in front of a house at a baptism celebration. Alex is thickly built, in his midtwenties, a handsome guy with tattoos stretching across his neck. His "tacks" on his chin and forehead are fainter than before. He's already undergone thirty-seven laser treatments (he needs, oh, say, ninety-six more). He is a simple guy and never did well in school. At a Dodgers game once, after singing the "Star Spangled Banner," with his hand over his heart, Alex confides, "You know, I couldn't tell my right hand from my left—if it weren't for the Pledge of Allegiance."

Since we're heading to the White House, I figure these guys can't exactly show up at the West Wing wearing size 85 waist Dickies. We head off to the Men's Wearhouse—"You're gonna like the way ya look—I guarantee it." (Well, that guy was nowhere in sight.) No sooner do we step into the Men's Wearhouse in Burbank than every salesperson in the place rushes us at the door as if to say, "How may we help you leave our store as quickly as possible."

"We'll be needing some suits," I tell them, pointing to the homies, "They're going to the White House for dinner."

If "eyes rolling" registered on the Richter scale—this is "The Big One."

They are quickly dispatched to dressing rooms. I'm idly

checking out ties, when Alex silently appears and stands in front
of a six-sided mirror. Alex, of the face covered in tattoos and the
heart covered in, well, nothing—you can get right to it. He's in a
suit. Alone, mouth open, he's staring at himself. He's hypnotized
by the guy in the suit in the mirror.

Alex's job at Homeboy is to help supervise our part-time
workers in their maintenance tasks around the headquarters.
Mainly, though, he gives tours. Reluctant at first to do so, Alex
has come to inhabit this role with a certain degree of delight and
his own particular brand of panache. He'll greet you at the front
door, introduce you to the job developers, explain our release
program, and hand you goggles so you can watch tattoos being
removed on the premises. He gives a good tour. Blessed are the
singlehearted. Jesus meant Alex. Few hearts come as true and
pure as Alex's.

I approach him with the same caution I would use with a deer
in the forest.

"You okay?"

His eyes don't meet mine; he's transfixed.

"Damn, G," he says, doing what can only be described as a jig,
"I'm already pinching myself."

Like he can't believe he's in a suit—and that the guy in the suit
is headed to the White House.

A week before we're scheduled to fly to DC, I call Alex into
my office.

"By the way," I ask him, "did you get permission from your
parole officer to go to Washington?"

Alex makes a face and pushes my question aside.

"'Course."

I indicate a general sense of "whew." There's a brief pause, and Alex says with a renewed timidity, "Um, well . . . yeah . . . she said no."

"WHAT?" I'm incredulous. "When were you going to get around to telling me this?"

"Well, actually," he says, completely defeated, "I wasn't gonna tell ya. 'Fraid ya wouldn't let me go."

I tell him to sit down.

"Look, *mijo*—we gotta do this the right way."

With him seated there, I get his parole agent on the phone.

After I lay out, gently, the details, ramifications, and importance of this trip to her, she listens and then says only, "No, high control." High control is what it sounds like. Alex is deemed to be a parolee requiring more vigilance and a shorter leash. This gets determined by a mixture of previous crimes, length of prison terms, and general past behavior. I ask to speak to her supervisor, who tells me, "Nope—high control."

"Is there someone," I ask, "who is, you know, a notch above you in the chain of command?"

I am put on hold for some time until the third official declares, "No way—high control."

They all seem to be having a very bad case of "And Alex, who exactly do you think you are—that *you* get to go to the White House . . . for dinner."

Many flying faxes from the Department of Justice and numerous pleas from the First Lady's office later—finally—the day before we are slotted to leave, we secure approval for Alex.

The morning of our departure is "Mishaps R Us." All the homies are late, and so we find ourselves stuck in the morning rush traffic. To no one in particular, I ask the homies in the car, "Y'all have your ID's?"

Silence. A lone voice (Charlie) from the back seat speaks, "Shit." We go back.

Two days later, on Thursday, the day they sport their suits for the conference and the White House dinner, we discover that poor old Alex has lost his pants. As near as we could piece together after the fact (and after Alex ran through my brother's house in DC, yelling, "I GOT NO PANTS"), it no doubt happened while he was running to my car in the early morning darkness. He had his gym bag slung over one shoulder and his Men's Wearhouse suit, covered in plastic, open at the bottom, placed over his other shoulder. Most likely in the excitement and haste to get to my car, the movement had jostled the pants on the hanger and dropped them on the sidewalk or in the gutter, where surely a homeless man is now liking the way he looks—I guarantee it.

My sister-in-law MacGyvers a pair of my brother's pants, and we're good to go to the conference and then the White House.

At the White House, butlers walk the halls carrying long-stemmed glasses of white wine on silver trays. The homies snatch those puppies *de volada*. Every room—the Blue Room—the Green Room—all those different colored rooms, seems to have either an elegant combo of musicians or a brass band. The Gold Room holds the buffet. Never in my life have I seen or tasted more exquisite food. I go back three times. Rack of lamb—perfection. A salmon the size of a duffle bag. Pastas, salads. They have these small, white potatoes, cut lengthwise, with a hole carefully bored and filled with caviar garnished with a sprig of chive. I'm standing with Alex as he pops one of those suckers into his mouth. And almost as quickly, with his discretion valve turned off, he spits the potato mess into a napkin and says, "THIS SHIT TASTES NASTY." His volume turns heads, and perhaps it was my imagination, but it sure seems that the Secret Service lunges, ever so slightly, in our direction.

The next day we head home, and somewhere in midflight Alex says he needs to go to the restroom. I point to the back of the plane.

Forty-five minutes later, Alex returns to his seat.

"Oye, qué pasó, cabrón—I thought you fell in?"

"Oh," Alex says, with his signature innocence, "I was just talkin' to that lady over there."

I turn around and see a lone flight attendant standing in the back.

Alex winces a bit.

"I made her cry. I hope that's okay."

"Well, Alex," I brace myself, "that might depend on what you actually said to her."

"Weellll," Alex begins, "She saw my Homeboy Industries shirt and tattoos and, weellll, she started to ask me a gaaaanng a' questions, so . . ."

He pauses with a whiff of embarrassment.

"So, I gave her a tour of the office."

At 34,000 feet, Alex walks this woman through our office. He introduces her to our job developers, explains our release program, and hands her goggles to watch tattoos being removed.

"And I told her that last night we made history," he says, with brimming excitement.

"For the first time in the history of this country, three gang members walked into the White House. We had dinner there . . . I told her the food tasted nasty."

He pauses and gets still.

"And she cried."

I get still myself.

"Well, *mijo,* whaddya 'spect? She just caught a glimpse of ya. She saw that you are somebody. She recognized you . . . as the shape of God's heart. Sometimes people cry when they see that."

Suddenly, kinship—two souls feeling their worth, flight attendant, gang member, 34,000 feet—no daylight separating them. Exactly what God had in mind.

* * *

If you locate one job for one homie from one gang, be assured that eight other homies from that same barrio will call asking for a job. It was in late May 1996 that Chico called. I didn't know him, but I had just found a job for one of his *camaradas.*

"Kick me down with a *jale,*" he blurts out with what I think is a fair amount of nerve. This roughly translates as: "Do you think you'd be able to locate gainful employment for me?"

"Well," I tell him, "I don't even know you, dog. How 'bout we meet first?"

I schedule a time to go to his house, which is not far from my office, situated on a steep, hilly street behind Roosevelt High School. Chico is sixteen and from a neighborhood whose roots reach back to the forties and the Pachuco (Zoot Suit) era.

I meet Chico's mom, Rosa, a sweet, diminutive woman who clearly delights in her children and maintains, at the same time, an evident dread at the path her bald-headed, *cholo* son has chosen. Her appreciation at my arrival this day is palpable.

Chico and I sit on the front porch. He is a lanky, funny-looking kid. As with most homies, his *pelón* haircut has pointed large arrows at his overly large ears, though his ears are more pronounced than most. His smile is ready and willing, always hanging out at the surface and quick to appear at the slightest urging. Chico is shy and jittery and yet will leap into areas of conversation that would take more time with other homies. We talk about his lady, his family, and his barrio's status with neighboring enemies. A most likable kid, made all the more winning by his nervy request for a job, sight unseen.

"So, if I got you a job, *mijo*, is there some skill you've always wanted to learn or pick up?"

Chico is quick. He needs no time to consider my question.

"Oh yeah, computers. I really wanna learn and know computers."

I assure him that I will work on this, promising only that I'll do my best.

Some days later, I call Chico. My investigation led me to the Chrysalis Center, a nonprofit homeless resource center in downtown Los Angeles. I knew that they had recently received a bank of computers, so I made them an offer. I told them I knew this kid, Chico, who wanted to learn everything there was to know about computers. He's a gang member, but he wants to redirect his life. He goes to school in the morning, I explained, and could work at the Center from 1 to 5 p.m., Monday through Friday. I tell them that I will pay his salary each week, and all they need to do is supervise him, teaching him everything they know about computers. We will call this a job.

They agree.

"Now, *mijo,* you start at one o'clock," I tell Chico over the phone, laying down the ground rules.

"If you don't go to school that morning, please don't bother to go to work either. And I'll know if you ditch school. A job is a privilege. Going to school every day makes you worthy. You will have two bosses. One of them you'll meet on Monday, and the other you're talkin' to right now. So if I find out, and I will, that you're hanging, banging, or slanging, with all due respect and love—I will fire your ass. Got it, dog?"

"I understand, G," he says, "*Oye, gracias.* I promise I won't let you down."

When one o'clock on Monday arrives, I stare at the clock on my wall. I think *Chico is now walking into the Chrysalis Center.* When it's five o'clock, I think, *Chico is now leaving the Chrysalis center.* I think maybe he'll call or stop by, so I stay in the office for some time. No word from Chico. On Tuesday, I repeat the same conscious staring at the clock and await a word or a visit from Chico after hours. Tuesday turns into Wednesday, Wednesday into Thursday. Still nothing. I start to think that maybe he flaked out on me. Maybe my directions were bad and he never found the place, too ashamed to call me. Maybe his probation officer popped him for something and his embarrassment keeps him from contacting me.

I have imagined all the possible scenarios and ponder Chico's failure to communicate, when on Thursday at 3 p.m., a message emerges from the fax machine next to my desk. I can spot at the top of the paper, the tiny, typed Chrysalis Center masthead. The fax is a missive from our man Chico, written in large, clumsy, script:

DEAR G:
I AM LEARNING HOW TO USE A FAX MACHINE.
I AM LEARNING A GANG A' SHIT HERE.
LOVE,
CHICO
P.S.: I REALLY LOVE THIS JOB
THANKS FOR GETTING IT FOR ME.

About two months later, as I fumble with the keys to my office door at 7:30 a.m., I hear the insistent ringing of the phone inside. I catch it midring. It's Chico's mom, Rosa. She tells me that the night before, Chico was standing with some friends, not far from his front porch. A car slowly crept up. Maddogging glances were exchanged. Windows were rolled down, words were volleyed back and forth, and, finally, bullets began to fly from within the backseat of the car. One of the bullets lodged very high up on the back of Chico's neck, and he is now in the intensive care unit at General Hospital.

I leave immediately.

I walk into the unit and see Chico lying there, skinny and tattooed, naked but for a diaper. He is heavily tubed, with all the requisite IVs—nose, mouth, arms. He is staring, most notably, wide-eyed and unblinking, at the ceiling, riveted to the acoustical tiles. There is a doctor at the foot of his bed, scribbling notes onto a clipboard. I go to him first to assess Chico's condition.

"You know, Father," the doctor begins, "In all my years, I've never seen a paralysis this high."

The doctor points to the back of his own neck.

"It is so high on the stem, that we suspect there may well be brain damage, though we're not certain."

The doctor leaves, and I walk closer to Chico. His eyes don't even register that I'm approaching. They remain transfixed on the ceiling, unblinking, stretched, it would seem, beyond their capacity. I lean in.

"Chico."

No movement, no acknowledgment at all. I anoint him in the Church's *unción de los enfermos*. I rub a generous swath of oil on his forehead, hoping against hope that the balm will penetrate his frozen state, hoping it will lead us both to some divine compensation for this mad, mindless waste of life. No such penetration happens. I am left thinking only, *menos mal*—just as well, that he not know what's going on.

Truth be told, this was a hard kid to visit the next day. Excruciating, really. After the first visit, a rush of memory swept through me and placed in bold relief the hugeness of this loss. I can still see Chico in my mind's eye, waiting for me on his front porch on a Friday afternoon. Unlike other homies waiting for their paychecks, I never had to honk my horn or leave my car in search of Chico. He was always there, seated on his porch, and I was almost always late. He would catch sight of my red car coming up the narrow, steep hill, and he would leap from the porch and head for my car in a hurry. He'd run this goofy, gangly trot (decidedly uncool—gang members don't run, unless law enforcement is chasing them). He had an absence of care about such things. He just wanted to get to ya (and get to ya he did). He would hop in the passenger side of my car, and there was no extricating him. He was there to stay and sit and talk. Gone long ago was the reticent shyness. He would just launch into it. He was, as we say, *bien preguntón*. He'd ask a grip a' questions. In fact, he'd invariably ask me stuff about God (like I would know).

"Is God pissed off if I have sex with my lady? What do you think heaven is like? Do you think God listens to us?"

Clearly, far more valuable than the measly paycheck I'd hand him every Friday afternoon was the time I was privileged to spend with him, in that car, wondering together what might be on God's mind. To this day, my only regret is that I didn't spend more time.

I did go back the next day, of course, to the hospital. I walked in and found Chico, much the same as I had the day before. But I made the attempt anyway.

"Chico," I say, not far from his ear. His frozen eyes thaw in an instant and they dart to my own, and they lock onto me and they will not let go. I'm startled by this and speechless. Chico's eyes become intense puddles. Mine do as well.

"Do you know who this is, *mijito?*"

And to the extent that he can nod affirmatively, he does so. If such a thing is possible, he nods his eyes.

I search for something, anything, to say.

"Do you know, *mijo,* that we all love you very much?"

This last statement sets him off, and he cries a great deal. He's wailing, really. And his face says to me, in a most unmistakable way, "Please . . . get me out . . . of this body."

I anoint him as I had the day before, and I think, *the good news is, he's alive.* The bad news now is that he knows enough to wish that he weren't. Our eyes cling to each other's as I finally leave him, slowly backing out of the intensive care unit. His eyes want to leap out of their sockets. They long to be transplanted anywhere else. I still see Chico's desperately haunted eyes after the door closes behind me.

One week later, Chico's heart stops, unable to sustain his ordeal any longer.

At the cemetery, as I bless the gold cross resting on his coffin and hand it to Rosa, a thought comes to me. I realize that I really must let this grief in. For too long, I had suspended my own profound sense of loss, dutifully placing it on my own emotional back burner. I needed to be there for Chico's family, his girlfriend, his homies. So I give myself permission now, to allow this pain into some cherished, readied place in my heart. Every homie's death recalls all the previous ones, and they all arrive at once, in a rush. I'm caught off guard, as well, by the sudden realization that Chico's burial is my eighth in the past three weeks.

I decide to walk away from the coffin and spot a lonely tree not too far from the crowd. I stand there by myself and welcome all the feelings of this great loss. I cry. Before too long, the mortician appears at my side. He is more acquaintance than friend.

Now he has broken the spell of my grief and unknowingly invaded the space I had carved out for myself. I am overwhelmingly annoyed that he has done so. Then, I'm annoyed that I'm annoyed. There is an obligation, clear and immediate, to break the silence, to welcome the mortician into my space, uninvited though he is. I remove my glasses and wipe away my tears. I point feebly at Chico's coffin and know that I need to find some words to fill our blank air.

"Now that," I whisper to the intruder, "was a terrific kid."

And the mortician, in a voice so loud and obnoxious that it turns the heads of all the gathered mourners, says, "HE WAS?"

My heart sinks. I know exactly what he's thinking. *No cabe—* something isn't fitting here; there is some large disconnect for him, and he's incredulous. How could it be possible that a sixteen-year-old *cholo,* gunned down, not far from his home, be a terrific kid?

But who wouldn't be proud to claim Chico as their own?

His soul feeling its worth before its leaving.

The mortician's incredulity reminds me that kinship remains elusive. Its absence asserts that any effort to help someone like Chico just might be a waste of our collective time.

"But in this place of which you say it is a waste, there will be heard again the voice of mirth and the voice of gladness . . . the voices of those who sing."

And so the voices at the margins get heard and the circle of compassion widens. Souls feeling their worth, refusing to forget that we belong to each other. No bullet can pierce this. The vision still has its time, and, yes, it presses on to fulfillment. It will not disappoint. And yet, if it delays, we can surely wait for it.

Acknowledgments

S t. Paul challenges us to "dedicate ourselves to thankfulness" and so I will.

I am deeply grateful to Hilary Redmon at Free Press for taking a chance on this book. Her clarity, compassion, and brilliant editing astonished me at every turn. Many thanks to Sydney Tanigawa for a faithful assist throughout. *Gracias* to production editor Kathryn Higuchi and the legal eye of Jennifer Weidman and publicist Christine Donnelly. David McCormick, my agent, always understood what this book wanted to be and made it happen. (Shout-out to Sally Willcox for introducing me.)

To my parents, Bernie and Kay, for showing me what "no matter whatness" really ought to look like. To my sisters and brothers, their spouses, nieces and nephews for the respite of laughter and joy.

I am thankful to the Society of Jesus for the home it has been since 1972, and especially to my brother Jesuits at Casa Luis Espinal, too numerous to mention. To my Provincial Superior, John McGarry, S.J., and the Superior of my community, Scott Santarosa, S.J., for their support and unshakeable trust.

Acknowledgments

I deeply appreciate the steadfastness of my board in guiding Homeboy Industries. Special mention must be given to Mike Hennigan and David Adams for ably chairing.

To my much beloved Council—Veronica, Mary Ellen, Quintin, Mario, Louis, Hectorious, Tin-Tin, Fabian, and Shirley. What an honor it is to delight with you in the blessing of Homeboy Industries.

To Ruben and Cristina, Paty, Kevin, Junior, and Anna for your friendship, leadership, and kindness in guiding our businesses.

Special thanks to Norma Gillette for her faithful service to Homeboy and for typing the earliest drafts of this book.

I am indebted to all the men and women who have served as staff at Homeboy over these twenty years.

Leslie Schwartz was the midwife of this book, nurturing and refining at a time when I sure had my doubts.

The fullness of gratitude in my heart goes to those friends who have never failed to walk with me over these years. The list includes some who read bits and pieces of this book and were positive enough, that I kept going: Tom Weston, S.J.; Tyler Hansbrough; Jane and Phil; Magonia; Peter Horton; Laura Chick; Tom Molettaire; Gary Yamauchi; Paul Lipscomb and Lynn; *mi primo* Tom; Charlie and Tina; Proyecto Pastoral; Cheryl and Mac; George Horan; Wendy Gruel; Rob and Joanne; Antonio, Emma, and Richard Mejico; the great Cara Gould (a veritable institution at Homeboy Industries); Javier and Jan; Howard Gray, S.J.; Joe and Rulis; Mike and Shelley; Joe and Angelica; Bebee; Diego and Polly; Don Smith; Bob Lawton, S.J.; Nick Pacheco; Claire Peeps; Hilda Solis; Gil Cedillo; Bob Hertzberg; Tom Carroll, S.J.; Kevin Ballard, S.J.; Tim Rutten and Leslie; the sisters at Whitethorn; Mark Ciccone, S.J.; Chick and Anita; Sr. Claudia;

Acknowledgments

Ed Reyes; Andy Alexander, S.J.; Culture Clash; Jim Hahn; Jeff and Catherine and the Catholic Worker community; Martin Sheen; Mary Nalick; Frank Buckley, S.J.; Jose Huizar; Sen. Barbara Boxer; Dick Riordan; Rich Grimes; Anjelica Huston; Robert Graham; Blinky Rodriguez; Antonio Villaraigosa; Robert Egan; Emily, Michelle, Santi, Pasky, Alison; Carlos and Luz; Carlos of IRS; Doug; Tom Smolich, S.J.; Theresa Karanik (OTI, PRGFF) and Alan; Ted Gabrielli, S.J.; Joan Harper; Jorja Leap (for saving me from parentheses and introducing me to Mark and Shannon); Mark Toohey, S.J.; Terry Gross; Gil Garcetti; the great and ever-faithful Carol Biondi; Sandra Ruth Diana; Bob Pecoraro, S.J.; Mike Kennedy, S.J.; John Lipson; Tom Brokaw; Fabian Montes; my "cuz" Kathleen; Marqueesi, for ironing board wisdom and debriefs at Paseo; Robert, for the unexpected phone messages; Becca; the Cusenzas; White Memorial; Eileen McDermott; Sr. Patricia; Alice and Jim Buckley; Eric Robles; the Maguires; Paul Miera; Buzz; Dennis Gibbs; Chris Ponet; "Sr." Patty Bartlette; Jamie, Ethel, and Kerry Kennedy; the legendary Mary Ridgway; Bo Taylor; Connie Rice; Ernie Martinez, S.J.; Ed Guthman; the Tortomasis; Steve Privett, S.J.; Greg and Lorenza; the Waldrons; Jim Grummer, S.J.; Mary Kay and Michael; Luis Rodriguez; Steve and Huey; Dennis Baker, S.J.; Paul Locatelli, S.J.; Brian and Lynn; Mike Engh, S.J.; Grant Dwyer; Tenny Wright, S.J.; Steve Soboroff; Tom and Lily; my Eastside hero Enrique; Pam Rector; Rick Cummings; Leonardo and Teresa; St. Louis Pharmacy; Bob Ross; Ray Stark; Fred Ali; Mark Ridley-Thomas; Zev Yaroslavsky; Don Knabe; Jose Ramirez; Gary Yates; Tom and Brigid LaBonge; Peter Byrne, S.J.; Wendy Stark; Vickie Rogers, Tom Hayden; Janis Minton; Nancy Daly; Nane; Alex Sanchez; Dr. Brian Johnston; Grover; Jim and Rob; Dave Mastroangelo, S.J.; "Haftrak";

Acknowledgments

Jeannette Van Vleck, C.S.J.; Mark Potter; Elias Puentes, S.J.; "Fulano de Tal"; Wallis Annenberg; David Price; Sonny Manuel, S.J.; Richard Atlas; Dorothy and Aliso Check Cashing; Mario Prietto, S.J.; Buddy and Sara; Barney Melekian; Laura Bush; Antonia Hernandez; Charlie Beck; Jeff Carr; Ellen Ziffren; Jane and Harry; Bill Bratton; Teddy; Eric Johnson; John and Carol; Walter McKinney; Myrna; Lupe Mosqueda; Brian O'Neil; Francis Porter; Mike Adams; Scott and Jeanie Wood; Sen. Paul Wellstone; Kathy Sanchez; the Lilligs; Paul Seave; Lee Baca; Ed Roski; Jackie Goldberg; Juan and Cuscatlan Optical; Romie; Ed Bacon; Arianna Huffington; Drs. Barnes, Kennedy, Khan, Mohrbacher, Pacino, and all the docs who remove tattoos; Jim Rude, S.J.; Bishops Gabino Zavala and Joe Sartoris; Fr. General Adolfo Nicolas, S.J.; My students at Folsom; John Woolway; Jack Clark, S.J.; Suzanne Jabro, C.S.J.; Jimmy McDonnell; Joe and Dora; Jimmy Blackman; Sr. Peg Dolan; John Bohm; *mi querida* Consuelo (HT); Joe and Deb; the nurses at Norris; Los Colonos de Islas Marias; Xochitl and the girls; the mothers of Dolores Mission and founding force of Homeboy: Teresa Navarro; Paula Hernandez; Rosa Campos; Rita Chaidez; Esperanza Vasquez; Lupe Loera; Sofia Guerrero; Maria Torres; Lupe Ruelas; Esperanza Sauma; Pam McDuffie; La Uva; and Yolanda Gallo; and all my *compadres, comadres,* and *aijados.*

Most especially to Al Naucke, S.J. ("And then . . . SF") for travels, pre–board meeting dinners, and embodying the care of the Society; to Bill Cain, S.J., for the gift of sharing "The Two Seasons" and revealing, always, the spaciousness of God's heart; to Jim Hayes, S.J., the best of friends, who calls me always to greater integrity and splendor; and to Celeste Fremon, for the gracious soul-friendship of our rhyming lives.

Acknowledgments

Finally, to the thousands and thousands of homies and home-girls, mentioned in this book and not. To know you has changed me forever and shown me *el rostro de Dios.*

It is to you that I dedicate my heart and this book.

For more information:
www.homeboy-industries.org
Homeboy Industries
130 W. Bruno St.
Los Angeles, CA.
90012
(323) 526-1254

About the Author

Gregory Boyle was ordained a Jesuit priest in 1984. He received his Master of Divinity from the Weston Jesuit School of Theology, a Master of Sacred Theology from the Jesuit School of Theology at Berkeley, and a master's degree in English from Loyola Marymount University. In 1988, Father Boyle began what would become Homeboy Industries, now located in downtown Los Angeles. Father Greg received the California Peace Prize; the Humanitarian of the Year Award from *Bon Appétit;* the Caring Institute's 2007 Most Caring People Award; and the 2008 Civic Medal of Honor from the Los Angeles Chamber of Commerce.

From 1986 to 1992, Father Gregory was the pastor of Dolores Mission in the Boyle Heights neighborhood of Los Angeles. The church sits between two large public housing projects, Pico Gardens and Aliso Village, known for decades as the gang capital of the world. There are 1,100 gangs encompassing 86,000 members in Los Angeles County, and Boyle Heights had the highest concentration of gang activity in the city. Since Father Greg—also known affectionately as G-dog—started Homeboy Industries more than twenty years ago, it has served members of more than half of the gangs in Los Angeles. In Homeboy Industries' various businesses—baking, silkscreening, landscaping—gang affiliations are left outside as young people work together, side by side, learning the mutual respect that comes from building something together.